VISUAL JIU-JITSU

The Art of Memorizing Techniques

WRITTEN BY

SHANE SMITH

Dedicated to the entire Gracie Jiu-Jitsu family.

Thank you for sharing your powerful art.

Contents

Introduction

The idea to share my jiu-jitsu learning methods came after listening to a Lex Fridman podcast on YouTube. The interview featured John Danaher and two of his famous martial arts students. For readers who have not heard of John, he is widely considered to be one of the greatest jiu-jitsu coaches of all time. He is a sixth-degree black belt under Renzo Gracie. One of his students on the podcast was Georges St-Pierre who is considered to be one of the best mixed martial artists of all time. The other student was Gordon Ryan who is currently considered to be one of the best jiu-jitsu competitors of all time. The fact that one teacher has coached two of the best martial artists in the world forced me to pay close attention to what he had to say about learning jiu-jitsu.

During the podcast John stated that the key to being successful in combat sports is to utilize an effective skill that is currently being undervalued and therefore underutilized by other competitors. In John's case he found that leg locks were highly effective, but they were rarely used in competition. Once he started focusing on teaching his students leg locks, they quickly started to dominate jiu-jitsu competitions.

His comment inspired me to write this book because I knew I had an effective skill that was currently being undervalued and therefore underutilized in jiu-jitsu. My undervalued skill is a powerful memory. If a jiu-jitsu practitioner could recall hundreds if not thousands of techniques under pressure, they would be the closest thing to a living jiu-jitsu cyborg we have ever seen. In October of 2021, John posted on Instagram that *"memory and retention are among the most important factors in your progress with jiu-jitsu."* I believe he is more than qualified to offer such constructive advice.

John Danaher also stated during another Lex Fridman podcast episode that he felt the primary skill that makes Gordon Ryan so much better than other competitors is his memory. He went on to state that Gordon has an uncanny ability to memorize new techniques very quickly. He said that he has never worked with a student who has had Gordons's degree of aptitude for memorizing techniques. John listed a few other skills and attributes that make Gordon Ryan so good at jiu-jitsu, but a powerful memory was listed first. This observation cannot be overlooked because a powerful memory is also the secret to success for world-class chess players.

In a study conducted by Gobet and Simon in 2000 it was determined that world-class chess players have over ten thousand chess moves memorized. They found that the main difference between an amateur chess player and a world-class chess player was in the number of moves they have stored in their memory. From 1984 until his retirement in 2005, Gary Kasparov was ranked number one in the world for a record 255 months as the World Chess Champion. Gary was twenty-two years old when he won his first championship, and he went on to dominate the mental sport for over twenty years. When he was asked to share his secret to success he responded, *"A good memory."*

It's no secret that the game of chess is very similar to the art of jiu-jitsu. Many jiu-jitsu practitioners rely on a couple of dozen techniques that they know really well. This is the equivalent of trying to shoot a clay pigeon out of the sky with a BB gun compared to using a shotgun with hundreds of BBs. No other martial art allows the practitioner to have time to think in the way that jiu-jitsu does. The ability to take someone to the ground and control their movement gives the practitioner time to use their memory to determine the next move. Jiu-jitsu is comprised of thousands of techniques with countless variations. This is how jiu-jitsu is like chess compared to other martial arts, which are more like checkers with a limited number of moves.

It's important to understand the organic process the body goes through when we learn jiu-jitsu. This will deepen your understanding of how our body can perform techniques that the brain has stored. It can be said that all athletic abilities start in the brain and work their way out to the muscles in our body. The first stage of learning a new jiu-jitsu technique requires mental recall. The second stage requires visualization. The third stage requires muscle memory, and the fourth stage requires strategic execution. If any part of the learning process is out of order it can and often does take many years to master jiu-jitsu.

Most jiu-jitsu schools jump straight into the third stage of learning by having the student practice a technique. They know that with enough repetitive practice the student will eventually memorize some of the techniques. This way of learning is inefficient because it often requires hundreds if not thousands of repetitions before a technique is stored in our long-term memory. That's why it takes around ten years to reach black belt. Some students will train for months just to be able to master a handful of techniques. Others will drop out of class entirely because they are so overwhelmed by all the techniques. Making the problem even worse, some schools do not have an organized curriculum. Instead, students must try and piece all the techniques they learn together until they eventually figure out how to apply them.

The jiu-jitsu community is already full of highly skilled instructors who can teach the third stage of learning techniques with practice. What the community is currently missing are instructors who can teach the first two stages of learning techniques with memory and visualization. When instructors start teaching their students how to memorize and visualize their techniques, the learning curve will be drastically shortened. This will allow more people to enjoy all the positive benefits this great art has to offer. Although I will be using jiu-jitsu techniques as examples throughout the book, the memory techniques you will learn are applicable to all martial arts.

The stories I heard of taking ten years to fully master the art of jiu-jitsu intimidated me at first. That seemed like a long time compared to other forms of martial arts. When I started to investigate the various forms of self-defense, I quickly realized how superior jiu-jitsu was compared to the rest of the martial arts I investigated. For so many years various forms of martial arts hid behind the smoke screen of effectiveness because they were never truly tested. It was easy for martial arts schools to seduce gullible students because they never had to demonstrate their martial skills in a real fight.

This all changed when the Gracie Jiu-Jitsu Academy started initiating public challenge matches with other martial arts schools. Hélio Gracie started the movement of validating jiu-jitsu when he publicly challenged anyone to fight regardless of their size. In 1932, when Hélio was eighteen years old, he fought his first professional fight against a boxer named Antonio Portugal. He won by armlock in less than a minute. He weighed 140 pounds soaking wet but went on to successfully defeat much larger opponents during his fighting career.

Another martial artist who demonstrated the effectiveness of jiu-jitsu was Hélio's son Rickson Gracie. Rickson has won numerous tournaments and championships. He has defeated fighters such as Japanese jiu-jitsu champion Yoshinori Nishi, kickboxing champion Bud Smith, Pankration champion Masakatsu Funaki, and Japanese wrestling champion Nobuhiko Takada. In 1980, Rickson cemented his legendary status when he defeated the famous vale tudo fighter Rei Zulu, who had a record of 140–0. Rickson racked up over four hundred wins with no defeats during his fighting career.

Although Hélio and Rickson paved the way for jiu-jitsu's popularity, it was Hélio's son Royce Gracie who may be the most famous in the family thanks to the UFC. The Ultimate Fighting Championship held its first event in 1993 at the McNichols Sports Arena in Denver, Colorado. The purpose of the UFC was to determine the most effective martial art in a tournament with minimal rules and no weight classes between competitors. The fighters represented multiple disciplines such as jiu-jitsu, boxing, kickboxing, wrestling, karate, taekwondo, sumo, judo, and more. The fighters had to win their first fight to advance to a semifinal fight. If they won their semifinal fight, they would advance to the final fight to determine the champion. All three fights took place on the same night with very little rest in between.

At the first UFC during his very first fight, Royce defeated a boxer named Art Jimmerson. He took him to the ground with a double leg takedown and obtained the dominant top mount position. Jimmerson quit by tapping out when he realized he could not escape from the position. In the semifinals, Royce defeated the much larger and stronger Ken Shamrock with a choke. Shamrock was over twenty-five pounds heavier than Royce at the time of the fight. Royce then went on to the finals to defeat the much larger karate and savate practitioner Gerard Gordeau by rear naked choke. This secured the championship win for Royce and demonstrated the effectiveness of Gracie Jiu-Jitsu for the entire world to see. After reading about the Gracie family fighting history, it's probably easy to see why I chose to study jiu-jitsu over the other martial arts systems.

I can offer the reader an inside look at a fairly unique method of learning jiu-jitsu. As a child my elementary school counselor labeled me as an autodidactic learner. In short, being an autodidact means that my brain will only accept knowledge that I have taught myself. When I want to learn something new, I must be able to understand the subject matter from the inside out. I have a hard time accepting facts at face value without understanding why they are a fact. This was very frustrating for my teachers in school. Can you imagine a kindergartner asking their teacher why they called an object by a name when the name is not the object? If my teacher had said: *"We use names for the sake of identification and communication,"* I would have accepted the need to call an object by a name.

My mind needs to understand why something is true before it accepts it as truth. It will not accept a theory, because in my mind a theory is an unresolved problem. The person proposing the theory has not solved the problem or it would be considered a fact. So, for me theories are a waste of time unless I can substantiate them with firsthand experience. I hope that by the time you finish reading this book you will have tested the visual jiu-jitsu learning method enough to determine if it is true for you.

Although some of my teachers in school called me a learning prodigy, I certainly didn't feel like one. One of the downsides of being an autodidactic learner is that if a subject does not interest me to an extreme degree, my mind will not be interested enough to learn about it. This is a major problem in school when you must learn about subjects that have nothing to do with your personal interests. Most of the population can force themselves to learn about boring subjects in school because they know they have to in order to pass the class. Unfortunately, my mind did not work that way as a kid. The harder I would try to remember boring facts, the quicker my brain would forget them.

Getting through prerequisites in college that have nothing to do with the skill or knowledge you wish to acquire is challenging for an autodidactic learner. If I had a really strong desire to learn the subject matter in a class, I would ace the exams and usually outperform the instructor who was teaching it. If I could not muster up enough desire to learn about the subject matter, I would fail the exams with the lowest score. I was either first in my class or dead last depending on the interest I had in the subject.

After growing sick of bad grades, I decided to learn how to force my mind to memorize boring facts. This led me to Dominic O'Brien who is an eight-time world memory champion. Dominic, like me, had to face learning challenges in school so he taught himself how to memorize anything. He was entered into the *Guinness World Records* in 2002 for memorizing a random sequence of 2,808 playing cards (fifty-four packs) after looking at each card only once. He was able to correctly recite their order, making only eight errors. After I learned all his memory techniques, I was able to overcome many of the negative aspects of being an autodidact.

In addition to learning memory techniques from Dominic O'Brien's book *How to Develop a Perfect Memory,* I have also learned many effective techniques from world-class chess players. The main difference between memory competitors and chess players is that chess players need to memorize moves in their long-term memory, and memory competitors only need to remember things for a short period of time. Another major difference between the two is that chess players need to memorize strategies that involve memorizing steps. Although they both use similar memory techniques, chess players use techniques that are more beneficial for jiu-jitsu practitioners. The only challenge in learning from chess players is that most of them keep their memory techniques private. Good luck getting a world-class chess player to share their memory techniques. Most of them want you to believe that they do not even use memory techniques, in the same way that many world-class jiu-jitsu competitors do not want you to believe they take steroids. Luckily for you, I have already breached their veil of secrecy, and will share many of their memory techniques openly throughout this book.

Memory was once my biggest fault, but now it's my strongest asset. Memory techniques allowed me to master over three hundred jiu-jitsu techniques in less than thirty days. What I accomplished in a few weeks takes most students many years to achieve. Memorizing hundreds of jiu-jitsu techniques in a month may sound impressive, but it's nothing compared to world-class chess players who have over ten thousand moves memorized. Jiu-jitsu practitioners have a long way to go to catch up with the mental faculties of world-class chess players.

In the event you find yourself injured or your body is unable to perform jiu-jitsu techniques due to age, visual jiu-jitsu is an excellent stand-alone practice. Just memorizing and visualizing the techniques in our mind allows the neural pathways in our brain and body to stay active. This will allow us to maintain our jiu-jitsu skills while we continue to learn and expand our mental jiu-jitsu library. Hélio Gracie was still performing techniques in his nineties. Neither age nor injuries should ever be an excuse not to continue evolving our jiu-jitsu skills.

This book was not written to teach you jiu-jitsu. It was written to teach you how to learn jiu-jitsu. The memory techniques you will learn in the following chapters can drastically shorten your learning curve. The ability to memorize hundreds of new techniques in a short period of time is well within your reach. Once you learn how world-class chess players memorize thousands of moves with ease, you will quickly realize how easy it is to learn complex jiu-jitsu techniques in a very short period. Not only will you be able to learn jiu-jitsu techniques faster, but you will also be able to retain what you have learned and apply it under pressure.

If you watch a jiu-jitsu match with two highly skilled competitors, you will notice how many times they get stuck in a stalemate. Each competitor knows how to counter the move that the other is attempting. It's a race to see who can remember what to do next. Most competitors have learned their techniques through repetition, so the memories of their techniques are scattered throughout their minds in no particular order. The first competitor who gets lucky enough to have the right technique pop into their mind wins. When a jiu-jitsu match gets stalled, you can see the competitors' mental wheels turning, but nothing is being done. This is why the sport of jiu-jitsu is often boring for people who do not practice it. With an organized mind, there will be less stalling and more fluidity to matches. This will please the fans because there will be more action during the match. When the fans of jiu-jitsu are happy, the sport will continue to flourish.

Becoming proficient at remembering techniques in an orderly fashion will demystify the learning process for you. When you memorize a technique, the principles that make it work should become clear to you. When I first started learning jiu-jitsu, I was amazed at how many techniques there were. It was like visiting a foreign country and not being able to speak the language. Once you memorize enough techniques you will be able to speak the language of jiu-jitsu. At first you will only be able to speak in words when you memorize the names of techniques. However, if you keep at it, you will learn how to speak in sentences as you memorize the steps of a technique. After you memorize enough sentences, you will be able to speak jiu-jitsu fluently with your training partners. A deeper look into this learning process will be covered in the next chapter.

CHAPTER 1

Visual Jiu-Jitsu Method

Visual jiu-jitsu consists of several distinct stages of memory development. The first stage consists of memorizing technique names using memory techniques such as the loci method, association, chunking, mind maps, and repetition. The second stage consists of memorizing the steps of a technique using detailed notes and linking stories. The third stage allows us to clearly visualize the technique with ordinary and extraordinary visualization. The fourth stage connects our brain to our muscles by practicing the technique solo and with a training partner. The fifth stage allows us to create a strategy to use the techniques we have memorized. The sixth stage and beyond are beyond the scope of this book but may be written about in the future.

One stage of memory development builds upon the previous one. Without being able to mentally recall the technique you will not be able to practice it. If you do not practice the technique, you will not have the muscle memory needed to physically perform it. If you do not physically perform the technique, you will not have the conditioned reflexes needed to execute your strategy. If you leave even one stage out, your jiu-jitsu skills will be underdeveloped and therefore incomplete.

When I want to learn a new skill, the first thing I do is research the skill as thoroughly as possible. I try to gather as many facts about the skill as I possibly can before preparing a strategic plan to master it. The first thing I did when I decided to learn jiu-jitsu was to research the most effective schools and teachers. After months of careful research, I narrowed my choices down to just one martial arts school and one additional instructor. The school was GracieUniversity. com and the additional instructor was John Danaher via BJJFanatics.com. Gracie University provides me with effective self-defense techniques and John Danaher provides me with effective sporting techniques. Together, I'm equipped with both self-defense and sporting skills. This has proven to be a well-rounded curriculum for me based on the goals I have for jiu-jitsu.

There are a lot of people who feel the sport of jiu-jitsu can be used for self-defense and I agree with them to a certain extent. The main difference between self-defense jiu-jitsu and sporting jiu-jitsu is that the sport of jiu-jitsu does not factor in strikes. Gracie University primarily focuses on techniques that prevent strikes and address real-world self-defense scenarios. As someone who understands the importance of muscle memory, I believe you must train with strikes in jiu-jitsu in order to maintain the myelin sheath around the neural pathways that the brain uses to block strikes. That being said, a lot of self-defense jiu-jitsu practitioners will get submitted rather quickly by a sporting jiu-jitsu practitioner. When you remove the threat of strikes, a higher level of jiu-jitsu opens up.

Gracie University is now run by Rener and Ryron Gracie who are grandsons of Hélio Gracie. This was the first Gracie Jiu-Jitsu school in the United States. Its main campus is now located in Torrence, California, but it was started out of a garage in the 1970s by Rorion Gracie. Rorion is the eldest son of Hélio and the father of Rener and Ryron. He is also the cofounder of the UFC. Gracie University is the same school that both Rickson and Royce Gracie taught at when they first moved to the United States from Brazil. In addition to having certified training centers all over the world they also have a comprehensive online school.

The decision to sign up for online classes allowed me the convenience of watching videos at my own pace. This granted me the freedom to apply my own learning methods to master their primary techniques. Rener and Ryron saved me a lot of time because they had already condensed their white belt program down to just thirty-six lessons that consisted of nearly eighty techniques and variations in total. Normally this is something I must do myself when I learn a new skill. In addition to providing an efficient self-defense curriculum they also provide extremely detailed lessons. This is another key detail that saved me a lot of time.

The art of jiu-jitsu is filled with thousands of techniques and is growing every day. It would be nearly impossible for the average person to learn every technique and effectively use them in a real street fight. Rener and Ryron had the clarity of mind to realize this, so they simplified their belt system. They designed their white belt program around techniques that they used to teach the military. This condensed system of jiu-jitsu was originally created to get soldiers ready for combat in the shortest period of time. They developed the system by reviewing past fights and challenge matches the Gracies had won over the years. The techniques that were used most often in real street fights were chosen to be included in the program.

Upon successful completion of the white belt curriculum the student is awarded a Gracie Combatives belt. This belt is still a white belt, but it has a stripe of blue down the center of it. It signifies that the student is prepared to defend themselves in a real street fight as long as the opponent does not have a higher degree of skill in jiu-jitsu. The fact that people with colored belts in jiu-jitsu make up less than 99.9 percent of the population, it's safe to say your odds are good at being able to defend yourself once you have earned the Gracie Combatives belt.

Once you have earned your first belt you can then start climbing the jiu-jitsu ladder. The second belt you will be able to earn is the blue belt followed by purple, brown, black, coral, and red. Coral and red belts take nearly a lifetime to earn and are only awarded to distinguished masters. It takes approximately eight to twelve months to earn the Gracie Combatives belt. It will take another six to twelve months to earn a blue belt. After blue belt, it will take approximately three to four years for purple belt, and an additional three to four years for brown belt. Altogether, it will take around ten years to earn a black belt.

Those are the time frames Gracie University estimates for the average dedicated student. To my surprise, I was able to learn all their basic white belt techniques in a little over a week using memory techniques. Not only did I learn how to perform the techniques, but I also had them memorized forward and backward. The techniques became a part of my mental real estate. Even though it's been a couple of years since I first learned those techniques, I can still summon them back into my awareness at will. Many jiu-jitsu students forget a technique almost as fast as they learn it.

After I memorized all the basic white belt lessons, I went on to memorize all sixty of their blue belt stripe one lessons.

Those lessons consisted of over two hundred techniques and variations. I set a goal to learn at least three new lessons each day and some days I would even exceed that. Most of the techniques in their blue belt stripe one course are additional variations and counters to the techniques taught in their white belt curriculum. This made it extremely easy to remember the techniques because I had already created the mental folders for them in my first mind map. You will learn more about mind maps in the next chapter.

These fundamental techniques have formed the foundation for all the other techniques I have learned to date. The art of jiu-jitsu relies strongly on the intellect. Just learning the techniques can immediately prove useful in a real street fight. This is one of the main advantages of this art. In a short period of time, a jiu-jitsu practitioner has a distinct advantage over a much larger untrained opponent.

Not everyone will have an ample amount of time to dedicate to memorizing techniques. It may take you several weeks or even months to memorize three hundred techniques. You will need to go at your own pace as time allows. Back when the Gracie Academy started in Brazil, they taught their white belt techniques one at a time over a period of forty lessons. Each student had a private one-hour lesson with an instructor. They did not begin instructing group classes until they started teaching in the United States. Hélio wanted to prepare his students to defend themselves in the shortest amount of time possible. His solution was to teach one lesson at a time in a precise order so that after forty lessons the student would be ready to defend themself.

After I purchased the Gracie Combatives course, I scanned through the lessons to see how I wanted to format my training regimen. My method of self-learning requires me to fully understand the end goal before breaking down the smaller, detailed goals. I quickly realized the end goal was going to involve learning a lot more than thirty-six lessons. Each lesson may contain multiple variations of a technique depending on the circumstance. Whenever I learn a skill that involves multiple facets, I incorporate memory techniques. These techniques allow me to recall hundreds of details in a very short period of time.

I consider the name of a technique to be the mental folder and the steps of a technique to be the mental files. World-class chess players call this technique *chunking*. By chunking large amounts of information into smaller mental files, it allows us to recall the details of a technique more efficiently. Once I memorize the name and order number of a technique, I turn my attention to the smaller details of the technique. This is a crucial step in my learning process. I must be able to paint a mental picture of what the instructor is trying to demonstrate. Just watching the technique being performed does not store it in my memory. I must see it in my own mind using visualization. This allows my mind to accept what they are teaching once I can see it for myself. This also allows me to learn the technique from the inside out.

In order to achieve this, I have to shift from a student to a teacher. I must figure out how to teach myself what the instructor is trying to teach me. If I'm not successful with this step my mind will dismiss what they are teaching, and it will not be absorbed into my memory. My mind will only hold on to what it can visualize, and it will automatically discard the rest. It's during this second stage of my learning process that I get to see if I'm actually going to be able to learn a new skill or not.

The tool I apply to create a detailed mental image involves taking notes. I must break the technique down into very small parts and I use detailed notes to do that. The number of parts I write down determines the clarity of the mental image I will be able to create. The clearer the picture of the technique is in my mind, the easier it will be to visualize in the next stage of memory development. When I watched the first video lesson on Gracie University's website, I broke down a fairly simple technique into many small parts. I then had to formulate notes to help anchor those parts in my mind. Now when I read my notes from that first lesson, I'm able to clearly visualize what it should look like instead of trying to remember what it looks like. Visualization is in the present moment and memory is in the past. I use my notes from the past to help evoke a present picture in my mind. It's the difference between remembering what someone looks like compared to looking at a picture of them. The picture was taken in the past but it's in your present field of awareness as you look at it.

When we visualize a technique, the clarity falls short of actually performing it, much like looking at a picture of Hawaii is not as clear as actually walking on the beach in Hawaii. The clarity of a picture in photography is determined by the number of pixels or micro parts it has within its borders. Each part of the jiu-jitsu technique that we can clearly visualize counts as one pixel. If we want our mental image to be clearer, we must add more pixels to it. The average mind only wants to record in low resolution because it's more efficient to do so. This causes the mental image of the technique to be fuzzy at best. But if we slow the observation process down and look at one small part at a time, we will eventually form a mental image that is in high definition. This ability to add as many pixels as we can to a mental image is the key to what people call a photographic memory. Some people are born with this ability, but I had to work hard for it. After we break a jiu-jitsu technique down into small parts with notes, it's time for the next stage of memory development.

The next stage involves creating a linking story that allows our mind to paint memorable pictures of the technique so that we don't forget it. When we break down the details of a technique with notes, we draw a basic black-and-white picture of it in our mind. Now we need to paint the mental picture of the technique by overdramatizing each step using colorful and emotive images. For example, instead of trying to remember the step of a technique that involves us grabbing the opponent's arm with a full grip, we would visualize our hand turning into a bear trap that clamps down on the opponent's arm. Now instead of just remembering the physical act of grabbing the opponent's arm we have a dramatic picture of a bear trap to anchor to.

Once we have created a colorful visualization, we need to link it to the next step of the technique. For example, when we perform the trap and roll escape technique, we first trap the opponent's arm, then we trap their leg. The way we can link the two steps is to visualize a bear trap clamping down on their arm. Once the bear trap clamps down on their arm it punctures their skin and honey sprays out of their arm instead of blood. The honey sprays all over the opponent's leg and it causes our leg to get stuck to their leg. This would complete the second step of trapping the opponent's leg. Then we would link being stuck to the opponent's leg with the next step of the technique.

Memory champions have been using linking stories for decades. It's one of the most popular memory techniques for recalling smaller details in the proper order. Once we can recall all the steps in a technique with a linking story, we will be able to link it with the name of the technique. When we can remember the name of a technique and all its steps, we are ready to visualize it with clarity in our mind.

The second stage of visual jiu-jitsu involves visualizing the technique with a virtual training partner. We must be able to visualize a sparring session with so much clarity that our mind is tricked into thinking it's real. Many scientific studies have been performed on Olympic athletes to determine the effectiveness of visualization. One study hooked athletes up to an EEG machine to measure their brain waves. They then had the athletes physically perform their sport. After they measured their brain waves while performing the sport, they had the athletes visualize playing the sport. The athletes' brain waves responded in the same way to visualization as they did when they actually performed the sport. You can do a quick search online to see how many Olympians use visualization. Nearly every Olympian has visualization as a part of their training regimen for a reason. **Ref. 11**

After the first two stages of visual jiu-jitsu are complete, we need to develop the third stage, which involves developing muscle memory with solo drilling. This allows us to perform the technique without a training partner. We simply go through the motions of the technique. After we feel comfortable with our ability to perform the technique solo, we need to practice the technique on a grappling dummy. This provides a more realistic feel compared to just going through the physical motions. We start out slow, but gradually practice the technique at a more realistic speed.

Visualizing techniques create neural connections in our brain, but drilling solo helps us connect those nerves to the muscles in our body. Our nerves are surrounded by a fatty cellular sheath called myelin. Myelin is used to insulate our nerves and helps to prevent a nerve signal from misfiring. Once the outer coating of myelin is thick enough, the nerve is fully insulated and can carry out a neurotransmission from the brain to the body very quickly. This process is most commonly referred to as *muscle memory*. In order to perform a technique under pressure, our nerves have to be fully insulated with myelin. You will learn more about myelin in future chapters.

After drilling solo for a while, it's time to move on to training with a partner. Once we start to feel fairly fluid with a technique, we need to practice with a willing training partner to drill the technique. We need to play the role of attacker as well as defender so that we can see the technique from both sides.

The fourth stage of visual jiu-jitsu involves creating and memorizing strategies. After you have memorized a sufficient number of techniques, you will be able to develop a game plan to put them into action. You will start with a simple strategy and build outward to include numerous contingencies. You basically create a plan for a plan based on every situation you may be confronted with. The more complex your strategy becomes, the harder it will be for your opponent to defend against it. This stage of memory development is where the masters of jiu-jitsu reside.

CHAPTER 2

Memorizing Technique Names

In 2020, *Scientific American* magazine published an article called "The Brain Learns in Unexpected Ways." In the article it outlined how the brain learns by coding memories with a protective sheath of white matter called myelin. White matter is the insulation that surrounds our neural pathways, and it plays a critical role in memorizing jiu-jitsu techniques. Prior to the discovery of myelin, the scientific community relied on outdated theories to explain the learning process.

One of the first theories on how the brain learns dates back to Ivan Pavlov's famous dog experiments. He found that dogs could learn to salivate at the sound of a bell. In 1949 psychologist Donald Hebb adapted Pavlov's *associative learning rule* to explain how brain cells might acquire knowledge. Hebb proposed that when two neurons fire together they send off impulses that cause the connections between the synapses to grow stronger. He theorized that when this occurs a memory is formed. Researchers would later discover that strengthening a synapse cannot produce a memory on its own. We now know that a memory can only be formed when our conscious awareness is linked to a sense impression with a protective sheath called myelin. **Ref. 1**

Pavlov's dog experiments proved that a dog's brain learns when it associates the sound of a bell with the presence of food. What they failed to discover was that it was myelin that was responsible for the dog's learning to associate the bell with food. Every time they rang a bell and the dogs observed food, a small amount of myelin surrounded that neuro-association in the brain. The association between the bell and food is called a memory. If we do not have something to associate a sense perception with, we cannot remember it long term. Instead, the sense impression would be stored in our short-term memory. This would cause the memory to fade away as soon as the myelin sheath breaks down. **Ref. 5**

In order for us to remember a jiu-jitsu technique efficiently we need to be able to associate the new technique with an old memory that is already stored in our long-term memory. Practitioners who rely on repetition to remember techniques are only accessing their short-term memory. Eventually during a random training session an association will be made that will allow them to store the technique in their long-term memory. It could be a sound or a specific look that creates the association, but something connected the dots, and the association was made. Most people describe this as something "clicked." The person could have been practicing the technique for months and then one day something clicked, and they got it. The part that clicked was the technique finally established an association and was transferred from the short-term memory located in the brain's hippocampus to the long-term memory located in the neocortex. **Ref. 6**

To test this theory, close your eyes and visualize your favorite jiu-jitsu technique. What did you see? In order to remember a technique, you have to be able to see it in your mind. You probably visualized your training partner getting submitted by the technique. To visualize the technique, you had to first know what technique to choose. Once you chose the technique, you were able to visualize all the mental images that are associated with it. In order to choose a technique, we have to be able to identify it. In order to distinguish it from all the other techniques stored in our mind we give it a name. Now that we have a name for the technique, we can attach all the associated memories to it. This allows us to replay it in our mind. This will become extremely important once you start practicing the memory techniques in this book.

When we learned how to walk as a toddler it was not from watching others perform the task. We first learned how to walk based on the instinct to move. Our DNA is encoded with the instincts needed to initiate the urge to move at a certain stage of our development. Once that DNA sequence was activated in our brain we started to learn how to roll over onto our stomachs. We instinctively knew as babies that we could not move if we were on our backs. Once we figured out how to turn over onto our stomach the race was on. The next step in learning how to move was to crawl. After we spent some time crawling another instinct became active and we wanted to move faster. This is when we learned how to stand up. Just like a baby learns to roll over as the first stage of movement, they also learn that standing up is the first step that leads to faster movement. Once we learned how to stand up, we learned how to take a few steps before falling. Slowly over time our brain started to communicate with our body more efficiently and we began to walk and eventually run. If you pay close attention to how we learned to move as children, you will clearly see that each step of learning was first activated by an instinct in the brain. After the brain initiated the instinct to move, the urge was expressed with our body and we began to learn how to move. This is why I start by teaching the brain a new skill before practicing the skill with my body. **Ref. 12**

The first stage of teaching the brain a new jiu-jitsu technique involves memorization. The learning advantage we now have that we didn't have as babies is the power of memory. From the beginning of the human race, we have been sharing skills with others in the hope of evolving as a species. Jiu-jitsu is no different than any other skill that has evolved over time. The jiu-jitsu masters of the world have already created thousands of techniques and they are creating more every day. Instead of trying to reinvent the wheel each time we practice jiu-jitsu, we can save a lot of time by memorizing techniques that have already been created. This will allow us to equal or surpass the instructors who are teaching the techniques. In order for us to take full advantage of the evolutionary shortcut called *memory*, we need to learn as much about it as possible.

Most of us know about short-term memory, working memory, and long-term memory. The ones you might not know about are spatial memory and visual memory. Short-term memory allows us to hold on to a small amount of information for a few seconds before we lose it. An example of this would be remembering someone's telephone number. Working memory allows us to hold on to information a little longer so that we can manipulate it in order to solve a problem like arithmetic. Long-term memory is unique in that it can be stored in the brain indefinitely. **Ref. 3**

Spatial memory allows us to remember the direction, distance, and location between objects. Without spatial memory we would not be able to navigate our surroundings. The three main components of spatial memory consist of the direction we need to go, the distance we need to travel, and the landmarks we need to look out for. In 1994 Hermer and Spelke determined that when toddlers begin to walk, they navigate by their sense of the world's layout. This allows the toddler to know where the walls in their room are by developing a mental map of the space around them. They were able to demonstrate that the hippocampus in our brain is active at a very early age. The hippocampus provides us with a spatial map of our environment. It allows us to know where the boundaries are so that we can know our location in space. The hippocampus is closely associated with short-term memory, but it also plays a key role in retrieving long-term memories from the brain's neocortex. **Ref. 4**

Tapping into spatial memory has allowed memory champions to remember thousands of new names in a very short period of time. Most people can only remember a few new names for about five seconds before they forget them. When we tap into our spatial memory, we can store memories for an extended period. This is because spatial memories are the connecting link between short-term memories and long-term memories. That's why we can remember trips we have taken years later. We can remember certain aspects of the route we took and the major landmarks we observed along the way. We only made the trip once, but we can remember it for the rest of our lives. How many of us can say that we saw a bunch of new jiu-jitsu techniques one time and we remembered them years later? Tapping into this unique aspect of spatial memory can make it seem like we are jiu-jitsu prodigies.

One of the unique aspects of spatial memory is the ability to remember landmarks. If we were to look at an unknown landmark on a random postcard, we would not be able to connect a link to it. Without a link to the landmark, we would not be able to remember it long term. Spatial memory provides a link to the memory of a landmark by using the route we traveled to see the landmark. Each landmark we see on a trip connects a dot from one landmark to the next. If we were to see only the last landmark on the trip, we would not be able to connect the dots in our mind to retrieve that memory at a later date. The bridge from our conscious awareness to the last landmark we want to remember is created from numerous landmarks along the path of our trip.

The memory techniques you are about to learn use mental landmarks from your imagination and connect them along a specific route that is already stored in your long-term memory. The origination of this technique dates back to the ancient days of Greece. Before paper and pens existed, the ancient Greeks had to rely on heavy clay tablets to write down notes. This made it nearly impossible to give long speeches based on notes. Instead, the orators of the time had to rely on their memories. They devised a mnemonic memory technique called *the method of loci*. The Latin word *loci* means "places." The word *mnemonic* is a memory term that is used to describe ways to encode a memory with more meaning in hopes of retaining it in our long-term memory.

The method of loci was once considered a secret that was only shared with the high-ranking elite of that era. If a politician possessed the ability to memorize speeches that lasted for hours, they were considered worthy of office. Even back then a strong memory gave the appearance of mental prowess and intellectual superiority. Now just about anyone can run for political office because they can read cheat sheets and teleprompters. Although some people may claim they invented this memory technique, history shows that it has already been around for thousands of years. **Ref. 91**

The last category of memory you need to learn about is visual memory. It's no secret that the mind's primary way of recalling memories is to use mental pictures. The old saying "A picture is worth a thousand words" is very true when it comes to the mind. The brain's most efficient way to store memories is by using mental images to form landmarks. Each mental picture contains thousands of small details. The name of a jiu-jitsu technique can be considered the picture frame, and the steps of the technique can be considered the picture. Before we can remember the steps of a technique, we must first memorize its name. The memory techniques we use to remember the steps of a jiu-jitsu technique will be found in a later chapter. Right now, you need to create a mental folder before you can store files within that folder. The mental folder is the name of the technique, and the files are the individual steps of a technique.

If you do not have a name for a technique, you will need to create your own. I had to do this with many of the techniques I learned from John Danaher. John will often go straight into demonstrating a technique without having a name for it. This is a good thing for the student because it gives you the freedom to name it yourself. This makes it even easier to remember the technique because you're using your own words.

For us to learn a jiu-jitsu technique in the shortest period of time, we must first transform the name of the technique into a mental picture. Once we have a picture that spells out the name, we need to place it along a familiar route inside our home. We need to start the route by facing the front door. Once you step into your front door the first object that is located on the left side of the door is considered the first technique. If you have more than one object on the left side of the door, you start with the object that is closest to the ceiling and work your way down. You will always want to work from left to right in your house. If you have a room on the left side of the house, enter the room and choose an object that is on the left side as soon as you enter the room. Then work your way all the way around the room until you exit the room and move on to the next location in your house.

Each object you can recall from memory will represent one technique. Each variation of the technique will appear from top to bottom and left to right on the same object. For example, the trap and roll escape name is at the top of my primary bedroom door. The left side of the door represents the punch block variation, and the right side of the door represents the headlock variation. This allows me to know the technique name as well as all the variations of the technique in one location.

The objects you choose should be easy to remember. This allows the mental picture of the technique's name that is stored in your short-term memory to become associated with an object that is stored in your long-term memory. The more times you have seen the object, the thicker the myelin sheath will be and the easier it will be to recall. The number of items you have in your house will determine how many techniques you can store inside of it. If you run out of space, you can always use another house that you previously lived in. You're only limited by your imagination.

You should not practice the technique yet because you need to plan out the mind map of your house very carefully. If you test the technique too hastily, you will end up developing associations that may be problematic when you actually start the process of creating your virtual jiu-jitsu house. I call this burning a house. A burnt house is when we experiment with the technique and develop an association in the virtual house that will be replaced later by a permanent association. This creates two competing images at the same location and can cause the desired association to become tainted. Right now, I'm just providing you with an overview of the technique so that you will understand how it works in relation to spatial and visual memory.

When I first started memorizing jiu-jitsu techniques, I used the house that I was living in to create a mind map. I didn't know at the time that I would have an interest in learning hundreds of techniques, so I only designed it to hold a limited number. This worked really well, and I was able to quickly remember all of the Gracie Combatives techniques, but I also burned part of the house. When I realized that I wanted to learn hundreds of techniques, I had to carefully squeeze them into the rest of the house. I eventually had to start using houses that I previously lived in to accommodate my ever-evolving jiu-jitsu library. It's always best to use the house you are currently living in for your first mind map. This will allow you to take pictures of the house and refresh your memory on a daily basis. Once your mind map is stored in your long-term memory it does not matter if you stay living in the house.

Now that you have a basic understanding of what a mind map is, it's time to discuss the process of converting a jiu-jitsu technique name into a mental image. I'm going to use an example from the first lesson I learned from Rener and Ryron Gracie. The first lesson is called *Trap and Roll Escape*. I used my bedroom door to associate the name of the technique with. The top of the door was the name of the technique and the sides of the door made up the variations.

For example,

1) Trap and Roll Escape (top of primary bedroom door)

   Visual: A dinner roll is stuck to a flytrap that is attached to a fire escape on top of the door and it's being blown around by the wind.

a) Punch Block Variation (left side of primary bedroom door)

Visual: A cheerleader punches a concrete cinder block with her pom-poms on the left side of the door.

b) Headlock Variation (right side of primary bedroom door)

Visual: A cheerleader has a padlock around her neck on the right side of the door and she is desperately trying to unlock it.

c) Open Guard Pass (bottom of primary bedroom door)

Visual: A British guard pushes the bottom of the door open and passes through the doorway.

I use a mnemonic memory technique for the word *variation* because I think of a cheerleader with her arms up in a V formation. If you combine *V* with *ation* I think of variation. As you read my sample mind map in the appendix, you may not clearly understand why I choose the words I do. You are the only one who needs to understand your visuals. What makes sense to me may not make any sense to you. The word *variation* makes me think of a cheerleader, but it might make you think of the word *vibration*. Both words are similar, but one might be easier for you to remember than the other. A cheerleader is easy for me to remember but something vibrating is not.

It takes less than a minute to create a mental picture and associate it with a location. That's how long it takes to store a technique name in our working memory. After recalling the image and location a couple of times each day for a week it will be stored in our long-term memory. Once the technique is in our long-term memory, we can truly say we own it. It can be called upon at will any time we need it. In order to keep a clear mental image of a technique name, it's a good idea to recall it in the morning after you wake up and shortly before going to bed. This helps to preserve the myelin sheath around the memory. Recalling hundreds of technique names from memory is also a powerful form of meditation. This practice can prepare our mental faculties for advanced visual jiu-jitsu practices that far exceed the scope of this book.

Now you can see how memory champions remember hundreds of names in a matter of minutes. This also gives away their secret of being able to recall the order number as well. When you learn this way it's just as easy to remember the forward order number as it is the backward order number. Then you can truly say that you know the technique forward and backward. If someone were to ask me what technique is taught in the Gracie Comabtives third lesson, I would start at the first object in my house and count from left to right until I got to the third object, which represents the *Positional Control from Top Mount* techniques. If someone asked what technique is taught in lesson thirty-three, I would count backward three objects from the thirty-sixth lesson. Eventually you will become so efficient at locating techniques in your mind that you will no longer need to count up or down to find them.

One of the best mind maps to learn the art of jiu-jitsu involves creating seven distinct sections of a virtual house. As I mentioned earlier, my first mind map used one section of my house to store all thirty-six lessons from the Gracie Combatives course. The second mind map I created stored all my blue belt stripe one techniques. Looking back this was a mistake, but I was able to correct it when I started expanding my mental jiu-jitsu library. You are free to organize your mind map any way you want. I have selected the most effective mind map as an example for you to consider. I now have seven separate sections of my house to store all my techniques in. Body position determines what part of the house my techniques are stored in. This allows my mind to know which section of the house to go to in order to recall techniques from the position I'm in during a fight or sparring match.

The first section of my house stores standing techniques. The second section stores guard techniques. The third section stores leg locks. The fourth section stores top mount techniques. The fifth section stores side mount techniques. The sixth section stores back mount techniques, and the seventh section of my house stores the principles of jiu-jitsu. To learn more about the principles of jiu-jitsu, I recommend reading Rener Gracie's book *The 32 Principles*.

In each section, the first techniques listed are offensive, while the second set consists of defensive techniques. Top positions are considered offensive and bottom positions are categorized as defense. For example, if I have twenty techniques in a room for one body position, the left half of the room will be for offensive techniques, and the right half of the room will be for defensive techniques. The more organized our techniques are in our mind the quicker they can be recalled under pressure.

By grouping the techniques into seven sections based on body position, and further dividing them into offensive or defensive, you will be using a memory technique called *chunking*. Chunking is one of the primary techniques that world-class chess players use to memorize thousands of moves. When we take a large chunk of information and organize it into smaller chunks of information, we can access the information more efficiently. Our memory works based on associations so the more defined our chunks of information are, the faster they can be recalled.

I developed this mind map after watching John Danaher explain that there are four distinct stages of a jiu-jitsu fight. The first part of most fights involves standing on the feet. As a jiu-jitsu practitioner the first priority in a fight is to get the fight to the ground. Once we are on the ground, we must deal with passing the opponent's legs. The opponent can kick us from their back, or they can wrap their legs around us and establish guard. After we are able to pass the opponent's legs, we can then establish a dominant mount position. This will allow us to control the opponent. Once we have control of the opponent, we can then start to work on submitting the opponent by strangulation, arm lock, or leg lock. That is why I created seven separate sections of my virtual house. Each part is laid out in the order they will be addressed during an actual fight. When I'm standing in a fight, I don't want to be thinking about submitting the opponent. I want to be thinking about how I'm going to get them to the ground. This is why the standing techniques are located in the first part of my virtual house.

Some readers may doubt their ability to create mind maps using mental pictures. I did as well when I first started. What I soon found out is that the more you use the right brain to create mental images the more active it becomes. It's like waking up a sleeping dragon within us. Most of us disconnect more and more from the right brain as we age. When we were kids our right brain was dominant and our imagination would run wild. As we got older the left brain became more dominant when we learned how to speak. Now in order to fully benefit from visual jiu-jitsu you will have to reverse the aging process by tapping into your childhood imagination once again.

In a recent study it was determined that distinguished memory champions' brains did not exhibit specific regional differences during resting periods compared to control brains. What they did find was that during active periods there were network connectivity changes in the memory champions' brains that were not observed in the control brains. When the control subjects trained for just six weeks using the same memory techniques found in this book, their brain connectivity became nearly identical to the memory champions brains. This study proves that all of us have the ability to optimize our memory and it can be done in a very short period of time. **Ref. 87**

During the 1960s, Roger Sperry conducted an experiment on epileptic patients who had their corpus callosum surgically severed. The corpus callosum is the area of the brain that links the right and left hemisphere together. Sperry's experiment was based on flashing images in the right and left visual fields of his participants. Because the participant's corpus callosum was severed, the information processed by each visual field could not be transmitted to the other hemisphere. In one experiment, Sperry flashed images in the right visual field, which would subsequently be transmitted to the left hemisphere of the brain. When asked to repeat what they had previously observed, participants were fully capable of remembering the image that flashed. However, when the participants were asked to draw what they had observed, they were unable to do so. When Sperry flashed images in the left visual field, the information processed would be sent to the right hemisphere of the brain. When asked to repeat what they had previously observed, participants were unable to recall the image that was flashed but were successful in drawing the image. Based on this finding, Sperry concluded that the left hemisphere of the brain was dedicated to language as the participants could clearly speak the image flashed. On the other hand, Sperry concluded that the right hemisphere of the brain was involved in more creative activities such as drawing. **Ref. 7**

Sperry's experiment demonstrated the important role the corpus callosum plays in sharing information between our brain's hemispheres. It's interesting to note that Albert Einstein's corpus callosum at the time of his death was thicker than fifty-two young, healthy males who served as a comparison group. Einstein was seventy-six years old when he died, and his brain was donated to science. Numerous studies have been conducted on the anatomy of his brain but one of the most recent studies was conducted by physicists from East China Normal University in Shanghai and Florida State University anthropologist Dean Falk.

The authors of the study were particularly impressed by the relative size of Einstein's corpus callosum at the splenium. This is a region of the corpus callosum that facilitates communication among the parietal, temporal, and occipital lobes. It also affects the brain's intellectual command center within the prefrontal cortex. The parietal and occipital lobes play a large role in visualization and manipulating visuospatial information. They concluded the study by stating, "Our findings suggest that Einstein's extraordinary cognition was related not only to his unique cortical structure, but also to the enhanced communication routes between his two cerebral hemispheres."

Peter Tse, a Dartmouth College neuroscientist who recently explored the underpinnings of the study stated, "The ways in which we use our brains, and the consistency with which we do so, may matter more as we age. That might reflect the fact that Einstein continued to exercise his brain strenuously, forestalling much of the atrophy that comes with age. It might just be that Einstein's brain was more like a young person's brain in that sense. The brain is like a muscle in the sense that neural circuits that are used often tend to change in their organization. That, in turn, may lead to increases, or at least changes, in connective tissues such as the corpus callosum. We should therefore not conclude that Einstein's genius was caused by some part of his brain being slightly larger than average. It might be that his brain was slightly larger in these areas because he exercised these regions more than the average person." **Ref. 9**

In 1929 during an interview that was published in *The Saturday Evening Post,* Albert Einstein was asked what his secret to solving complex problems was. He responded, "I am enough of an artist to draw freely upon my imagination. Imagination is more important than knowledge. Knowledge is limited, but imagination encircles the world."

In order to efficiently learn jiu-jitsu techniques in the shortest period of time, you will need both sides of your brain to fire in harmony in order to fully express your inner genius. The martial aspect of jiu-jitsu is knowing the techniques with the left side of our brain. The artistic aspect of jiu-jitsu is creatively expressing the techniques with the right side of our brain. Most people rely on the left brain to learn and the right brain to express creativity. When you combine the two you will be able to learn and express creativity with both sides of your brain simultaneously. This will make the learning process seem effortless. The ancient martial artists called this *wu wei* and it was expressed with the yin-yang symbol.

CHAPTER 3

Creating a Mind Map

Now that you have a better understanding of why we need to create a mind map from the previous chapter, it's time to start the actual practice of creating and memorizing one. If you put the following steps into practice, you will quickly realize the power of the memory techniques involved.

Creating a Mind Map

1) **List Techniques:** The first step is to write out a list of all the technique names that you want to memorize. I was lucky because my jiu-jitsu school has its entire curriculum online. This allowed me to know in advance how many techniques I would need to learn. If your school does not provide a complete list of techniques for their curriculum online, ask your instructor if they will write them all down for you. You can also create your own names for the techniques your school teaches.

2) **Seven Sections:** Once you have a complete list of all the techniques you want to memorize, you will need to separate them into seven sections. The seven sections are standing, guard, leg locks, top mount, side mount, back mount, and principles.

3) **Offense/Defense or Top/Bottom:** Standing techniques and leg locks are divided into offensive and defensive techniques. Guard, top mount, side mount, and back mount techniques are divided by top and bottom instead of offense or defense. Top positions are often considered offensive positions and that's why I list them first.

4) **Subcategories:** In addition to dividing the techniques into offensive or defensive, you will also need to subdivide them into additional categories. This will allow the chunking memory technique to work more effectively. Start with all the standing techniques. Once you have all the standing techniques written down, divide the offensive techniques into clinches, takedowns, and counters. Then divide the defensive techniques into, standing front attack defenses, standing rear attack defenses, and standing weapon defenses. The guard techniques are further divided into guard passes, half guard top, guard submission counters, guard controls, half guard bottom, sport guards, guard submissions, and guard sweeps. The leg lock positions are divided into straight foot locks and counters, toe hold foot locks and counters, knee locks and counters, and heel hooks and counters. The mount positions are further divided into controls, submissions, submission counters, and escapes. If you train at Gracie University, they already have most of their techniques subdivided for you.

5) **Visual Route:** Now that you have a complete list of techniques that are divided into seven sections and further subdivided into their appropriate categories, it's time to create a visual route of your house. The best way

to do this is to take pictures of every room in your house and print them out. If you do not want to take pictures you can draw a detailed map instead. You will then number the objects in each room of your house starting from left to right. If you have more than one item in the same location list the object closest to the ceiling first and work your way down. Be careful not to select too many objects in a confined space. It will make it more difficult to see the visuals if they are crowded together.

You will need to know how many techniques you want to memorize for each section. This will allow you to know if you have enough objects in a room to fit all the techniques into. You may need to combine two rooms to have enough room. For example, you have twenty standing techniques you want to memorize but you only have fifteen objects in a room. You will need to continue to work left to right in your house until you have enough objects to fit twenty techniques into. It's always a good idea to leave extra objects in a room for additional techniques down the road.

If I want to memorize twenty techniques and the first room on the left of my house only has fifteen objects in it, but the second room on the left side of the house has another fifteen objects in it. I will only use five of the objects in the second room and leave the other ten objects for future techniques. When I start the next section of techniques, I will choose an entirely new room so that I'm not combining technique positions in the same room. If you have a small home, you may have to combine technique positions into the same room. You can also use another house that you can clearly remember, like a childhood home.

6) **Associate Object with Name:** Once you have all the objects numbered, you will need to write the name of the technique on top of the object in your picture or drawing. If the technique has multiple variations, list them from left to right under the technique name on the same object. Refer to the previous chapter or the appendix for examples. This physical map will serve as a backup for the visual map in your mind. You will rely on it heavily during the first week of training. At this point you should have all your technique names organized and a household object associated with each one.

7) **Associate Image with Name:** Now it's time to associate an image with the name of the technique. If your first technique is the *Trap and Roll Escape,* you can visualize a fly trap tied to a fire escape with a dinner roll stuck to it.

8) **Superimpose Image:** Once you have an image that spells out each word of the technique, you will need to superimpose that image over the object in your house. For example, visualize a fly trap being tied to a fire escape that is attached to the object in your house. Write this down in as much detail as possible for your records.

9) **Motion Picture:** The final step is to visualize your technique image interacting with the mental image of the household object. For example, visualize the fly trap swinging in the wind and getting stuck to the top of the household object. Adding motion helps to create a better memory. The crazier the motion picture is the better. Try to evoke as much emotion as you can with the picture in your mind. The stronger the emotion is the faster you will be able to recall it.

Memorizing the Mind Map

Once you have successfully created your mind map, it's time to start memorizing it. You will want to start with just one section at a time. Dedicate your first day of training to just memorizing standing techniques. Start with just the offensive techniques then move on to the defensive techniques of the section. Once you can remember both sections you will then start recalling them in reverse order. This will be easier than you think.

If you want to create a really large mind map it may take you much longer than a week. Work at your own pace, and never overdo it. Your mind will not be fully adjusted to the mental concentration you will need in the beginning. Give it time, and if you notice that you're feeling overwhelmed, you have gone too far for the day. Resume your training the next day and stop when you start to lose interest. You cannot force the right brain to work like you can with the left brain. It will retaliate and shut down if you try. The right brain is our inner child, and it wants to have fun. If you start forcing it to pay attention it will lose interest and the memory techniques will abruptly stop working. You want to avoid this at all costs. In the words of Ryron Gracie, *"Keep it playful!"*

Once you can recall your list of techniques forward and backward, you will want to start focusing on the fifth technique of each list. If you have sixteen standing offensive techniques, you will focus strongly on the first technique, fifth technique, tenth technique, and fifteenth technique. The reason you want to really point these techniques out more than the others is because they will help you locate techniques faster. It will also help you if you forget the number of a technique. You will be able to go back to the fifth, tenth, or fifteenth technique and start over from there instead of having to start over at the beginning of the list.

Once you feel like you can confidently recall all of your standing techniques forward and backward, it's time to move on to the next section of techniques the following day. When you start memorizing your next section of techniques always start with the techniques you memorized on the prior days. You worked hard to get the techniques stored in your mind, don't lose them now. Within one week you will have memorized all seven sections forward and backward. Every morning you should run through all your techniques forward and backward. It's best to do it again before you go to bed. If you're running short on time or your mind is too exhausted, you can go through the techniques in forward order in the morning and in reverse order at night.

The importance of mentally recalling the techniques in reverse order cannot be overstated. When we recall the techniques in forward order from left to right, we are engaging our left brain more than our right brain. When we recall the techniques in reverse order from right to left, we are engaging our right brain more than our left brain. This is why it will usually be easier for people who are naturally right-handed to recall the techniques in forward order from left to right. If you are naturally left-handed it may be easier to recall the techniques in reverse order. The left hemisphere of our brain controls the right side of our body, and the right hemisphere of our brain controls the left side of our body. **Ref. 8**

Leonardo Da Vinci is considered to be one of the greatest creative minds of all time. He had an unusual style of writing called mirror writing. He would write in reverse order as if you were looking in a mirror. This rare writing ability is closely associated with left-handed people or with people who have suffered strokes on one side of their brain. Da Vinci was left-handed, and he had also suffered a stroke. Theoretically, when we recall our jiu-jitsu techniques in reverse order, we are benefiting from the same natural ability Da Vinci had for accessing his right brain. Through a process of reverse engineering, we attempt to tap into a small spark of his creative genius. **Ref. 10**

Both sides of our brain must be able to recall the techniques with equal proficiency. This skill will carry over into a later stage of memory development when you visualize performing jiu-jitsu techniques from both sides of your body. Most of us will have a preferred side to work from based on our dominant hand. When you learn how to visualize a technique, you will start with your dominant side, then move on to your nondominant side. Once you can clearly visualize a technique from both sides of your virtual body you will be ready to practice the technique with your physical body.

You are going to surprise yourself with how fast you can remember technique names. Some people describe these memory techniques as miraculous because they never thought it would be possible to remember hundreds of techniques. The act of recalling so many techniques creates tremendous mental concentration. You will find that recalling your techniques becomes a daily meditation that not only keeps you proficient at jiu-jitsu, but it will also strengthen your mind.

You now have all the tools you need to create your own mind map. In the books I've read, memory champions and chess players often teach by sharing their own mind maps. I have adopted this practice as well. In the appendix, you will find the first mind map I created for jiu-jitsu. Hopefully viewing one of my own jiu-jitsu mind maps will give you a better idea of what your mind map might look like. It should only serve as a template because you need to use mental pictures that are unique to your own memory for the best results. If you have a really tough time getting started, you can always use my mental images until your imagination gets strong enough.

Our imagination is a lot like a muscle. The more you use it, the stronger and more active it will become. Remember to start with a limited number of techniques and build up from there. Trying to memorize hundreds of techniques right out of the gate is a quick way to exhaust your mental faculties. It can also damage the power of the memory techniques because the right brain will eventually revolt and shut down.

In Summary:

1) Write down all the techniques you want to memorize.

2) Organize the techniques into seven sections. Standing, guard, leg locks, top mount, side mount, back mount, and principles.

3) Subdivide each of the six body positions into offensive, defensive, top, and bottom.

4) Number the household objects in each section of your house from left to right and from top to bottom.

5) Designate a technique name to associate with each household object and list variations from left to right on the same object.

6) Create a mental image of the technique name and superimpose it onto the household object.

7) Add motion to your visual to make it easier to remember.

8) Memorize one section of technique names at a time without getting mentally exhausted. Start the next day by recalling all the previous technique names before memorizing more.

9) Recall all your techniques both forward and backward twice a day to maintain the myelin sheath around them.

CHAPTER 4

Memorizing Technique Steps

You should now have the names of your jiu-jitsu techniques stored as mental folders in your mind. Now it's time to create mental files consisting of the steps in the techniques. The memory techniques you will use to remember the individual steps of a jiu-jitsu technique are divided into two categories. The first category uses techniques that are focused on your intellectual left brain. Left brain memory techniques involve writing detailed notes.

Once you have written down the detailed steps of a technique, you will abbreviate your notes into a small paragraph. After you have condensed your notes down to the bare necessities, you will use a potent memory technique called *Fill In the Word*. This technique will make you look like a savant. When you can recite the steps of every jiu-jitsu technique you have ever learned, verbatim, it will be hard to deny your memory skills.

The second category of memory techniques is focused on your creative right brain. Right brain techniques involve creating linking stories. After you create a linking story, you will break it down into pictures that represent each step of the technique. This allows us to consolidate and encode the memory like we did with the left brain. Our left brain remembers in words and our right brain remembers in pictures. In order to remember your jiu-jitsu techniques under pressure, you will need to store your techniques on both sides of your brain. **Ref. 7**

The left side of our brain is largely associated with rational thinking and problem-solving. The right side of our brain is largely associated with processing emotions and responding to stress. In 2002 a study was conducted at Harvard University by Mark McManis, PhD, and Jerome Kagan, PhD. Their study demonstrated that activation of the right brain is closely associated with high reactivity and fearfulness. They discovered that the right brain has more control over the stress hormone system than the left brain does.

As Mike Tyson so eloquently stated: *"Everybody has a plan until they get punched in the mouth."* If we become injured in a fight, we run the risk of switching over to our reactive right brain. This is when our visual memory will help us to recall our techniques with linking stories. If we are casually drilling jiu-jitsu techniques with a training partner, we can easily remain in our left brain. Gordan Ryan is a good example of a jiu-jitsu competitor who is skilled at staying in their left brain as they compete. This is a skill that his coach John Danaher has praised in numerous interviews. Gordan can give his coach a play-by-play review of what he was thinking throughout the entire match. If he were to have been in his right brain, he would have only remembered a small number of details. Fighters refer to this as *blanking out*, because they go into a purely reflexive mindset due to fear and adrenaline. Once panic sets in, the brain is flooded with adrenaline and cortisol that is triggered from the right brain. This causes the left brain to shut down and become subordinate to the right brain. Instead of waiting for these stress hormones to clear out of our bloodstream, we can embrace the insanity, and recall our jiu-jitsu techniques with the right brain.

Some readers will be tempted to use only the left brain memory techniques because they are so effective. I would strongly encourage you not to make this mistake if you want to be a complete martial artist. Chess players can afford to memorize their techniques only in the left brain because they do not have to worry about a competitor trying to break their arm or choke them unconscious. Jiu-jitsu competitors do not have this luxury.

After you have memorized your linking story, you will need to link it to your technique name with a visual. This will allow you to remember the story as soon as you recall the name of the technique. Linking stories are made from visuals that represent each stage of the technique in sequential order. When you remember the first visual, the rest will follow like mental dominoes. When you finish your linking story, you will need to condense the story down to pictures that represent each step of the technique. This allows the memory to be consolidated and it will also provide the coding needed to recall the entire story based on a handful of pictures.

Once you're able to remember your techniques with words and pictures, you will use note cards to permanently store the techniques in your long-term memory. After the techniques are stored in your long-term memory, you will no longer need to recall them with memory techniques. You will simply recall the name of the technique and instantly remember how to perform it. This is the last stage of memory development and the first stage of visualization.

CHAPTER 5

Detailed Notes

In order to write detailed notes, you will first need to see what the technique looks like. Many of the jiu-jitsu techniques I have learned to date came from watching Rener and Ryron Gracie's instructional videos at GracieUniversity.com., as well as John Danaher's instructional videos at BJJFanatics.com. Without watching their videos, I would not have been able to formulate mental pictures of the techniques. If your jiu-jitsu school does not have its curriculum online where you can watch the techniques frame by frame, you will need to record your instructor demonstrating the techniques. This will allow you to play the videos back and formulate detailed notes based on each step of the technique.

This is what John Danaher had to say on Instagram about taking notes:

> Some learn and retain best with writing. That was always my favorite method. Even if you never read those notes again in your life, the mere act of focus and writing has a good clarifying effect on your thinking that will carry over into your grappling and overall thinking about the game. If you are ever injured and off the mats for a time, try writing as a temporary substitute for mat time and

see how much you can recall and how clearly you can expound it. You might be surprised at how it helps you when you return.

According to education experts at the Academic Success Center of Oregon State University, taking notes in class has two primary functions:

(a) It keeps you alert, attentive and accountable as you listen, and (b) the notes themselves become a record of what was said in lecture or discussion that can be used later for studying and review (Seward, 1910). According to Hartley & Marshall (1974) students who take notes experience increased attention and concentration in class (as cited in Cuseo, Fecas & Thompson, 2007). In addition, writing during class and reviewing notes before tests produces better recall which is important to your performance on exams (Kiewra, 1985). When evaluating your own note-taking strategies, ask yourself if you're achieving those two primary functions. If you aren't, consider ways you could alter your strategies to be more effective.

The first thing I do when I want to write down notes on an athletic skill such as jiu-jitsu is to watch the skill being performed without any explanation. When I started learning jiu-jitsu online, I would mute my computer while Rener and Ryron performed the technique. I would then write down every step I saw them perform in as much detail as possible. Once I felt confident that I had written down all the steps in the technique, I would then listen to them provide additional details about the technique. This gave me the opportunity to try and figure out the technique on my own before listening to them explain it. By trying to figure out the technique on my own, I was able to initiate a certain degree of accountability to learn the technique. This caused me to have an even greater appreciation for their instructions when I listened with audio. They were able to offer additional insights into the technique based on their lifetime of experience.

The problem with blindly accepting what an instructor has to say about a technique is that you never hold yourself fully accountable for learning the technique. You rely on your instructor to do all the work instead of taking it upon yourself to memorize and comprehend the purpose of the technique. Behavioral science calls this *herding*. Herding can be defined as the psychological phenomenon of following other people's information rather than following our own personal information. I call this *sheep mentality*, because you are relying on the instructor who is playing the role of shepherd. I believe in order to be successful at anything in life we have to assume the role of a shepherd, not a sheep. When you try to figure out what the steps of a technique are before hearing an instructor explain it, you are taking the first step in becoming your own shepherd. **Ref. 92**

My primary goal for writing down the steps of a technique is to form a mental image of what each step looks like. You will know if your notes are effective if you can visualize the technique just by reading them. I had very little knowledge of jiu-jitsu before I started to learn it. This handicap forced me to write down extremely detailed notes regarding each technique. For readers who are already familiar with jiu-jitsu they will probably be able to write down fewer steps. The primary goal of effective notetaking is to use a minimum number of words to describe a maximum number of details. If you don't have prior experience in jiu-jitsu training, you may need to take extremely detailed notes in order to see the technique clearly in your mind. I noticed that the more techniques I learned, the less detailed my notes became.

This was because I started to learn the principles behind each technique, which in turn allowed me to visualize new techniques with fewer words.

Following are two versions of the elbow escape technique from the bottom of mount. The first version was written from watching the instructional video on mute and the second version was written to give myself precise instructions based on my dominant side. In the second version I use right and left to help determine exactly what side of the body will be involved with the technique. Once I'm able to visualize the technique on my dominant side, I switch directions to visualize the technique on my nondominant side.

Elbow Escape Technique – Version One:

1) With the opponent mounted on top of you, place one hand on the back of the opponent, and hug them close to your body. This will prevent the opponent from leaning back and punching you.

2) Place your leg that is on the opposite side of your hugging arm flat on the ground. Keep your other leg bent with your foot flat on the ground to pivot off of. Turn your hips to the side facing away from your hugging arm by bumping your hips up slightly and pivoting on your foot.

3) With your free arm block the opponent's knee with your elbow. Use your elbow to slightly raise the opponent's knee off the ground so that your knee can slide under theirs. If your elbow is not long enough you can use your hand. Now bend your leg that is on the same side as your free arm north until it slides all the way under the opponent's knee. Return to your back and allow your free knee to face toward the sky. The opponent is now in half guard instead of full mount.

4) Trap the opponent's leg with the leg you just freed by crossing it over theirs. Hug the back of the opponent's neck with your arm from the same side of the body as their trapped leg.

5) Now block the opponent's knee on the other side of their body with your elbow or hand. Push off their knee and turn your hips sideways away from the opponent's knee you are blocking. This will give you enough room to pull your knee through to the inside of their leg. Return to your back with your lower leg still trapped by the opponent. Bend the trapped leg with knee facing up and foot flat on the ground.

6) Now switch arm positions behind the opponent's neck and establish stage one of the punch block series.

7) Place your free leg loosely around the opponent's back. Now pivot off the trapped leg until your hips turn sideways toward the direction of the trapped leg. This will allow you enough room to free your lower leg. Now swing your lower leg around the opponent's leg and return to your back. The opponent is now in your guard and you are free from the top mount.

Elbow Escape Technique – Version Two:

From the bottom of top mount, place your right hand on the opponent's back and hug them close to your body. Place your left leg flat on the ground. Keep your right leg bent with your right foot flat on the ground to pivot off of. Turn your hips onto your left side by bumping your hips up slightly and pivoting on your right foot. Now block the opponent's right knee with your left elbow or hand. Use your left elbow to raise the opponent's right knee off the ground and slide your left knee north under their right leg. Return to your back and trap the opponent's right leg with your left leg. Hug the back of the opponent's neck with your left arm. Then block the opponent's right knee with your right elbow or hand. Push off their right knee and turn your hips onto your right side. Return to your back and bend your right knee toward the sky in front of the opponent's left thigh. Now switch arm positions behind the opponent's neck and establish stage one of the punch block series from a three-quarter guard position. Place your left leg loosely around the opponent's back. Then pivot off your right foot as you swing your hips toward your right foot. Swing your lower right leg around the opponent's left leg and return to your back. Cross your feet behind the opponent's back to establish a closed guard.

I personally prefer to take notes using left and right directions. It minimizes mistakes and makes it easier to visualize the technique in my mind. Regardless of the style you use to take notes, it's important to use your own words to describe the steps in a technique. We all have a unique vocabulary that our minds are familiar with. When our mind recognizes familiar words being spoken to us, we experience a feeling of comfort and trust through the *mere-exposure effect*. The mere-exposure effect is a psychological phenomenon by which people tend to develop a preference for things merely because they are familiar with them. In social psychology, this effect is sometimes called the familiarity principle. The effect has been demonstrated with familiar words, paintings, pictures, shapes, and sounds. **Ref. 13**

To test this theory, the next time you are speaking with someone listen carefully to the words they are using. Then use some of the same words in your conversation with them. For example, a person says to you: "It's a wonderful day to go swimming." You would reply by saying: "It *is* a wonderful day to go swimming." Then you randomly select a few catchwords they are using throughout the conversation and subtly repeat the words back to them. You may be surprised to find that the person will not stop talking. At a subconscious level they automatically develop a rapport with you based on the familiar words you are using. You are literally *speaking their language*. I have tested this theory hundreds of times in my life. It's amazing how you can get a shy person to come out of their shell just by speaking some of their own words back to them.

Abbreviated Notes:

Now that you have watched the jiu-jitsu technique, and written down detailed directions, it's time to condense your notes. The key to successfully abbreviating your notes lies in the ability to write down just enough to recall the technique, and nothing more. If you can come back to your condensed notes a year later, and still be able to remember the steps, you will know that they are effective notes. This should be the litmus test for all your notes.

I'm going to provide an example of abbreviated notes from the first jiu-jitsu technique I ever learned. It's called the *Trap and Roll Escape* at Gracie University, but it's most commonly known as the *Upa*.

Detailed Directions:

> If the opponent has their right hand on your chest or throat, trap their right wrist with your right hand using a thumbless grip. Keep your right elbow tucked in as you trap the back of their right elbow with your left hand in a full grip. Now trap the opponent's right leg with your left leg and place your right leg inside of their left leg. Bridge your hips up and roll toward your left shoulder. Land on your knees in the opponent's guard with your head pressed down on their abdomen. Finish by trapping the opponent's hips with your elbows.

Abbreviated Directions:

> Trap their right wrist and tricep. Now trap their right leg and clear your right leg. Roll over your left shoulder and onto your knees. Press your head into their abdomen and trap their hips with your elbows.

You will notice that my abbreviated notes are very direct. The only reason they can be condensed down is because I first wrote the notes in full detail. Our brain learns best when it can consolidate details. This memory consolidation process is the act of learning. When we consolidate our notes, we are helping our brain remember the technique in the shortest time possible. The average person will be lucky if they can store one out of ten jiu-jitsu techniques in their long-term memory. When we abbreviate our notes, our success rate should go up to five out of ten. With the next technique you are going to learn, your success rate will go up to remembering ten out of ten techniques.

Fill In the Word Technique:

The last step of memorizing a technique with our left brain involves a memory technique called *Fill In the Word*. The previous step condensed the memory of the technique, but now we need to encode the memory to get it to stick in our long-term memory. I learned this technique from a four-time United States memory champion by the name of Nelson Dellis. He in turn learned the technique from an actress named Lauren Tothero. Memory athletes are a lot like jiu-jitsu athletes. Both communities freely share techniques among each other for the benefit of the sport.

Lauren discovered this technique when she wanted to be able to memorize an entire monologue on the spot. Most people do not give professional actors and actresses enough credit for their mental prowess. They are required to remember hundreds if not thousands of words in the exact order they were written. This is no easy feat. Not only do they have to memorize hundreds of words, but they also need to dramatize the words they are speaking. Memory competitors only have to focus on remembering the words.

The Fill In the Word technique is very simple, but its results are profound. As I mentioned earlier, this technique will make you look like a savant. You simply recall the name of the jiu-jitsu technique, and the steps will flow out of your mouth like butter. This memory technique involves writing down the first letter of each word in your abbreviated notes. You will capitalize the first letter of each sentence and use punctuation. The mind will be forced to fill in the rest of the word based on the first letter it sees. Once you successfully recall the correct word, just from seeing the first letter, you will know that your mind has encoded the memory. **Ref. 36**

I will use the Americana armlock technique to illustrate how it should look.

Abbreviated Directions:

> From the top mount position, pin their left wrist and elbow down. Place your left elbow on the ground. Slide your right hand palm up and grab your left wrist. Hook their right leg and brace with your right knee. Finish by dragging their left hand south.

Fill In the Word:

> F t t m p, p t l w a e d. P y l e o t g. S y r h p u a g y l w. H t r l a b w y r k. F b d t l h s.

You will need to read over your abbreviated directions a few times after you write down all the letters and punctuation.

Then you should be able to slowly recall the words from the letters. Once you can quickly recall the words from the letters, it's time to verbally repeat the directions without the letters. This will be your own personal savant moment. If you spent enough time on this practice, you should be able to effortlessly repeat your abbreviated notes, verbatim. You will not know where the information comes from in your mind. It does not come from a space in your mind like the names of the techniques do. You just have to accept the fact that the memory is there and run with it.

In psychology they refer to this as an implicit memory. There are two main types of long-term memories: *implicit memories* and *explicit memories*. Implicit memories are acquired unconsciously, and they explain why our brain can be primed to remember the rest of the word even though we only see the first letter. Explicit memories are acquired consciously when we write down the steps of a technique. When we read our notes, our explicit memory can recall the visual steps associated with the notes. When we recall our notes without looking at them, our implicit memory unconsciously feeds the steps to our conscious awareness. **Ref. 96**

The evidence to substantiate implicit memories arises in priming. Priming is the theory that exposure to one stimulus may influence a response to a subsequent stimulus. The most common way to determine the effectiveness of an implicit memory is to measure its performance. If you can recall a word after seeing just the first letter, you will know that the word is stored as an implicit memory. This will give you some confidence when it comes time to recite the steps of your technique. Even though we cannot consciously access our notes with this technique, we will know it works when the steps effortlessly roll off the tip of our tongues. This is also the litmus test for speaking a language fluently. When we can speak without thinking, we will know that the language is unconsciously stored in our long-term memory. **Ref. 97**

This memory technique is one of the most effective techniques I have ever worked with to remember notes and lines. The only aspect of the technique that I don't like is that I do not have conscious control over where the memory comes from. With spatial memory we have a specific location in our mind to look at. With this technique, it just appears of its own accord. In the next chapter you will memorize your techniques with linking stories. Linking stories have specific locations in your mind, because they are linked to the images of your technique names.

In Summary:

1) Watch a technique without listening to instructions.

2) Write down all the steps you see in the technique using your own words.

3) After you write down the steps, listen to the instructions for additional details.

4) Your notes should clearly form a mental image of the technique in your mind.

5) Abbreviate your notes and memorize them with the Fill In the Word technique.

CHAPTER 6

Linking Stories

Now that you have memorized your jiu-jitsu techniques with your left brain, it's time to memorize them with your right brain using a linking story. As I briefly mentioned in a previous chapter, a linking story allows us to paint memorable pictures of a jiu-jitsu technique in our mind so that we don't forget them. When we break down the details of a technique with notes, we are able to write black-and-white words about it in our minds. Now we need to create a mental picture of it by over-dramatizing each step using colorful and emotional images. The left side of our brain thinks in black-and-white words, while the right side of our brain thinks in colorful pictures. **Ref. 36**

In order to maximize our ability to remember the steps of a technique we need to convert boring words into exciting pictures. For example, instead of trying to remember the step of a technique that involves us grabbing the opponent's wrist with a full grip, we would visualize our hand turning into a metal bear trap that clamps down on their wrist. Now instead of just remembering the physical act of grabbing the opponent's wrist, we have a dramatic mental picture of a bear trap to anchor to. The more graphic the mental picture is, the easier it will be to remember.

Numerous studies over the years have demonstrated that a picture can be stored in our long-term memory after seeing it only once. One such study was published back in 2018 at the Frontiers in Neuroscience website. The study's objective was to determine how long it took for a picture to be stored in our long-term memory, but it revealed much more. The study demonstrated that it took only twenty milliseconds for 67 percent of the participants to form a long-term memory for a picture they had only observed once. The study went on to demonstrate that if the participants were briefly shown the same picture several times the success rate went up to 89 percent. **Ref. 15–16**

If our mind can remember a new picture after seeing it only once for a fraction of a second, how much more can it remember if we spend a few minutes looking at old pictures stored in our memory? When we use pictures from our memory to create a linking story, we increase the odds of remembering the story exponentially. Most of our mental pictures have been stored in our mind for most of our life. Even when we create a new mental picture with our imagination, we are still using details acquired from old memories to formulate it. For example, if I want to imagine a gorilla holding me down in a side mount position, the first mental pictures that flood my mind are from watching gorillas in the zoo or from movies that I have watched in the past. If I did not already have an image of a gorilla stored in my mind, I could not formulate a new picture of one holding me down. In addition to remembering what a gorilla looks like I also have to remember what the side mount position looks like. Then I can merge the two separate memories into one new image that will eventually go on to be stored as a memory. Creating new mental pictures out of old mental pictures is the key to imagination. It's also the key to remembering jiu-jitsu techniques quickly and efficiently. **Ref. 18–86**

Now that you understand the importance of using mental pictures to develop long-term memories, it's time to over-dramatize the motion of our mental pictures in order to create an even stronger memory. When we memorized the names of a technique, the mental images were fairly static. The images had a small amount of movement, but it was limited to the household object in our mind map. Now that we are memorizing the steps of a technique, it needs to involve a lot more activity. A study that was conducted in 2007 showed memories with motion were up to 300 percent more likely to be remembered long term than static images alone. **Ref. 88**

The act of adding motion to our linking story is the key to remembering it long term. Instead of just imagining a gorilla lying on top of you in a side mount position, have the gorilla do something bizarre. Perhaps the gorilla is juggling oranges or trimming its fingernails. Whatever it takes to get the gorilla moving will enhance our ability to remember the scene. The more motion we add to the mental movie, the better. You want to avoid static pauses in the linking story as much as possible. One scene should immediately link to the next scene. Our mind will then get used to looking for the next movement, which will also be the next step in the technique. One mental picture will lead into the next, giving the illusion of motion. The anticipation of the next step is what develops the neural connections in our brain. We are literally building a bridge from one memory to the next. **Ref. 17**

The closer we can associate one step in our jiu-jitsu technique with the next, the stronger the neural connection will be. For example, when I visualize the *body fold takedown* technique, the opponent throws a punch at me, so my arms turn into two pistols that I use to protect my face as I shoot into their chest. The opponent is wearing a steel toe boot on his front foot. The inside of my rear foot has a strong magnet on it that gets stuck to the outside of the opponent's front boot. My pistol arm that is closest to the opponent's back wraps around their waist. My other pistol arm turns into a monkey arm that grabs the end of the pistol barrel with a thumbless grip. My body now stands tall like a bear, and I bury my chest and head into the honey-covered chest of the opponent. I make sure that I'm always able to see the banana-themed watch on my monkey wrist. If I can't see the watch on my monkey wrist, I move my hips and head to face the direction of the watch. I lower my body like a frog getting ready to jump and I pull the opponent's waist in by pulling on my pistol barrel arm. The gun goes off because I squeezed too hard, and it startled me enough to lift the opponent up before falling forward on their body. As I'm falling to the ground, I bring my outside foot forward to slow the fall. My outside foot is wearing a turtle shell for a shoe. I also extend both of my arms out to brace with. Both arms have a red elbow brace on for support. I land on the opponent who is wearing a saddle, but I only have one foot in the stirrups. I quickly pull my other leg across the opponent and put my foot in the other stirrup to establish top mount.

One step of my linking story automatically leads into the next step. If I had not watched and written down the technique before creating the linking story, it would not have made much sense to me. Once we have converted our notes into colorful pictures and set them into motion by linking them all together, it's time for the next step.

The only thing missing in our story now is emotion. The way we feel about our linking story is what allows us to remember it. Unfortunately, negative emotions are easier to remember because they are connected to our brain's amygdala. The amygdala has been shown to play a primary role in the processing of memory, decision-making, and emotional responses such as fear and anger. **Ref. 89**

In 2006, renowned memory researchers Elizabeth Kensinger from Boston University and Daniel Schacter from Harvard University published a paper called "Emotional Memory Recollection." Their experiment focused on the memory of the 2004 American League Championship series of baseball where the Boston Red Sox defeated the New York Yankees. This game was chosen because it was widely considered an extremely emotional event. The study consisted of three categories. The highly positive Red Sox fans, the highly negative Yankees fans, and the neutral group who weren't fans of either team. The results showed that the highly emotional fans of the teams who won or lost remembered the sporting event better than the neutral spectators. The study found that emotional memory was recalled better than nonemotional memory. The study also found that the negative group of losing Yankee fans remembered more details about the game than the positive Red Sox fans. This is just one of many studies showing that negative memories are remembered more vividly than positive memories. **Ref. 90**

Although it may seem unpleasant to add negatively charged emotions to our linking story it will help to be able to remember the details of our jiu-jitsu techniques more efficiently. I have found that some techniques are easier to remember than others. If a technique is easy for me to remember, I do not add as much emotion to it. I save the emotion for techniques that have a lot of steps or are harder for me to remember. You will need to do the same with your own linking stories. It takes just as much time to create a warm and fuzzy story as it does to create a negative story. I know from personal experience that the negative story is easiest to remember. That's why some of my linking stories in the appendix will have a dark and sometimes morbid twist. I would rather remember the negative linking story in a dangerous street fight than forget it because I made it too positive.

For an example of making a positive step negative, see my linking story on the *Elevator Sweep* technique. The final step of the technique involves my leg chopping the opponent's leg out from underneath them. Instead of visualizing my leg as a chopstick in my linking story, I visualize my leg as a large butcher's knife. I associate a butcher's knife with chopping vegetables so it's easy to remember, but it also strikes an element of fear in me. I don't want to cut someone's leg, so it makes me cringe at the thought of it. That cringeworthy step is now deeply embedded in my long-term memory, and I know that it can easily be recalled in the heat of battle.

Fill In the Story Technique:

Now that you have completed your linking story, it needs to be consolidated and encoded into your memory in the same way your notes were. With linking stories, we condense the story down into pictures that represent each step. This allows us to consolidate the memory. The pictures also mimic the Fill In the Word technique, in that we will use the pictures to fill in the rest of the story. This technique allows us to consolidate and encode the memory at the same time. **Ref. 36**

Remember, pictures are to our right brain what words are to our left brain. This *Fill In the Story* technique is just as effective for our right brain as the Fill In the Word technique was for our left brain. The only difference is we need to visualize a picture and not a word. For example, when we write down the names of the pictures, we want to be able to imagine what the pictures look like. We don't want to visualize the word. One of the best ways to remember our linking story pictures is to draw them by hand. Drawing a picture activates the right brain, and speaking a word activates the left brain. The more active your right brain becomes, the easier it will be to remember the pictures. You will learn more about the importance of drawing in the next chapter.

I'm going to use the Americana armlock to illustrate what your linking story and pictures might look like. You can reference the appendix for even more examples.

Linking Story:

> The opponent is lying on their back and I'm sitting on a saddle that is cinched to their abdomen. Their left forearm turns into a bowling pin. I grab the neck of the bowling pin, which is the opponent's wrist and pin it to the ground with my left hand. I then use my right hand to press down on the base of the bowling pin, which is the opponent's left elbow. My left elbow now turns into a knife that I slice down the left side of the opponent's face. Now I let go of the opponent's left elbow with my right hand and my right arm turns into a monkey's arm. I slide my right monkey hand palm up under the opponent's left tricep and hook the top of my left wrist with a thumbless grip. I then hook the opponent's right leg with my left stirrup and brace with my right knee, which is wearing a red brace. I finish by dragging the top of the opponent's bowling pin right hand south along the ground.

Fill In the Story:

> Saddle, bowling pin, knife, monkey palm, stirrup, red knee brace, and bowling pin top.

As you can see, this exercise is very similar to the Fill In the Word technique. If you have spent enough time on this practice, you should be able to easily remember the whole story just from reading the names of the pictures and visualizing them in your mind. Once you can quickly recall the details of the entire linking story, just from recalling the pictures, you will be ready to recite the whole story from memory without looking at the pictures.

If you find that you're not able to easily remember certain parts of the story, you may want to rewrite those parts. Add more detail or provide more emotion to the pictures. The more creative your pictures are, the easier it will be to recall. For example, instead of just recalling a saddle, you will want to recall what type of saddle it is. Is it a Western or English saddle? Is it brown or black? Does it have silver conchos on it? You can also add fragrance to your image. Does the saddle smell like horse sweat? Does it smell like leather? The more questions you ask yourself, the more detailed the mental image will become. Once you can clearly recall the entire story, you will be ready to link it to the name of the technique.

Story with Name Association:

Grandmasters of chess have been using linking stories for decades. It's one of the most popular memory techniques for recalling smaller details in the proper order. Once we can recall all the steps in a technique with a linking story, it's time to associate the story with the name of the technique. In the very first step of memorizing the technique we used pictures to spell out the name of the technique. Now we need to add the first couple of pictures of the linking story to the name of the technique. We already know that the first picture of our linking story sets off the rest of the pictures like mental dominoes. This will allow us to add just the first one or two pictures from our linking story to the name of the technique. Then when we recall the name of the jiu-jitsu technique, we will automatically remember the first steps of the linking story. If the first steps of the linking story are too similar to other techniques, you can add multiple pictures from the linking story. You will be amazed at how quickly your linking story pictures stick to the original memory of the technique name.

The visual I use for the elbow escape technique from the bottom of mount is *a person leaning against a fire escape with their elbow while they sit on a horse at the top of the door.* The first couple of pictures of my linking story involve a bear's paw and a shotgun. The way I associate those images with my visual of the technique name is to imagine a bear shooting at the person leaning against the fire escape. I imagine the bear missing the person and hitting the door. Now when I recall the name of the technique, not only does it spell out the name of the technique, but it also shows me the first couple of steps of the technique. In addition to adding mental pictures of the linking story to the original pictures of the technique name, it also created more movement. This will make it even easier to remember the technique.

When you look at how long some of my linking stories are in the appendix, it might seem a little overwhelming. When we watch a good movie, we can remember it fairly easily. If we were to read the five-hundred-page script that the movie was made from, we would quickly lose interest. This is the same way a linking story works. When we look at how complex the linking story is, it makes it seem like it would be hard to remember. This could not be further from the truth. Once we visualize the story a couple of times, we no longer need to read the script because we can watch the mental movie.

Passively watching is much easier than actively reading. This is the secret to transferring our linking story from paper to the jiu-jitsu mats. The linking story becomes a movie that we can easily remember.

In Summary:

1) Convert your boring notes into an exciting linking story with negative emotions.

2) Select linking story pictures and memorize them with the Fill In the Story technique.

3) Associate the first couple of pictures of the linking story to the name of the technique.

CHAPTER 7

Note Cards

Now that you have memorized your notes and linking story, it's time to store them deep in your long-term memory. The most effective method I have found to mentally drill techniques involves four-by-six-inch note cards. Nearly all mental athletes have used note cards or flash cards at one point in their training. The ability to create an effective note card will determine your success with visual jiu-jitsu. Not only will they be used to transfer new jiu-jitsu techniques to your long-term memory, but they will also be used in a later chapter that involves memorizing strategies.

I have never observed a mathematical genius who did not write out their formulas on paper or a board. Albert Einstein had a preference for drawing on windows to get his ideas out. Whether you like it or not, you may be considered a jiu-jitsu genius by some of your peers, in the same way that many people mistake a memory champion for one. They will not be accustomed to seeing someone who knows so many techniques by heart. The decision to tell them your memory secrets will be yours to make.

The main difference between a natural genius and an artificial one is hard work. Not all of us were born with a two hundred-plus IQ, but we can create one where it counts. Just because we are not geniuses in math does not mean that we cannot become one in jiu-jitsu. How many people in your jiu-jitsu class are willing to use note cards to mentally drill techniques? Not as many as you may think. The fact that you're willing to take the time to use them shows that you have more tenacity than most. What you lack in natural genius you will make up for in hard work and perseverance.

Note cards allow us to measure our progress in a more external way. When we flash the name of a jiu-jitsu technique on a note card, we should be able to instantly recall its steps. If we cannot do so, then we know that the technique has not been stored in our long-term memory yet. This pass-or-fail assessment will go a long way in our memory development. If we cannot measure our current level of development, it will be all but impossible to monitor our progress and make changes when needed. This method of self-assessment is called *metacognition.*

Metacognition refers to being aware of our mental process and understanding the patterns that govern it. The term comes from the root word *meta,* meaning "beyond" or "on top of." Metacognition can take many forms, such as reflecting on our way of thinking or assessing our current level of memory development. When we evaluate our memory skills it is called *metamemory.* Metamemory is a type of metacognition that involves introspective reflection on our memory process. Being aware of our memory process has important implications for how we learn and use memories. When memorizing a jiu-jitsu technique, for example, we make judgments as to whether we have successfully learned the technique, and use these decisions, known as *judgments of learning,* to allocate our training time. **Ref. 98**

In order to get the most from our note cards, we need to organize them in a specific way to return the best results. Most four-by-six-inch note cards have ruled lines on the front and a blank back. You will need to write the name of the technique on the back of the note card. The first letter of the name should be written with a black pen and the second letter should be written with a red pen. Alternate between black and red letters for the entire technique name. This will force you to slow down and concentrate on your writing. Write as neatly as you can and focus on your spacing.

On the ruled line side, use a black pen to write your abbreviated notes on the top half of the note card. Then write down your Fill In the Word letters below your abbreviated notes. The final step is to draw your linking story pictures with a red pen at the bottom of the note card. Draw the pictures from left to right in the order they appear in the linking story. If you're not the best artist, just write the names of the pictures in red ink. The black pen represents the left brain, and the red pen represents the right brain. If you make a typo at any point in the process, start over with a new note card. This will encourage you to slow down and focus more carefully on your writing. The act of writing and drawing our notes by hand instead of using a computer has far-reaching benefits.

In 2014 a study in behavioral neuroscience was conducted by researchers at the University of California and Princeton University. The results of this study demonstrated that students who take notes by hand perform better with conceptual questions than students who record notes on computers and digital devices. According to the study, writing with a pen and paper allows us to summarize and organize information with our own word font. This encodes our memories in a more active and natural way. In contrast, the use of electronic devices inclines students to write passively. Another study in Japan reported that taking notes by hand improves students' memorization and word recognition. One of the main advantages of handwritten notes is that reading and writing on note cards improves our ability to memorize techniques. **Ref. 98**

Assuming you have already completed your first note card, it's time to develop a training regimen. Much of the memorization process has already been completed in the previous steps. Note card drills are the final step of memorizing a jiu-jitsu technique. This is where we get to find out if we truly know the technique by heart in our long-term memory. In the beginning you may be slow at recalling the steps of a technique, but with consistent practice, you should be able to recall them without hesitation.

In order to be precise with our metamemory assessment, we will use a stopwatch to determine how long it takes to recall the steps of a technique. The moment you read the name of the technique you will start the timer. You will stop the timer the moment you finish speaking the last word of the technique. Then you will write down the time in a training journal. You should write down the date and time of the exercise, so that you can monitor your progress. You will only time your abbreviated notes. You can take as much time as you need to recall the linking story as long as you do not miss any steps. You can also fluctuate your words as long as you get all of the pictures correct. You will start the drilling session with your abbreviated notes and end with your linking stories. This provides the best assessment of your current memory skills.

I prefer to keep my memory drill sessions brief but frequent. I will drill a technique three or four times, then wait a few hours, and do it again. We do not get much benefit from the drilling session after we can quickly recall the steps. You will need to let some time pass before you start another drilling session. If you ace the recall quickly on your first attempt, wait a few hours or wait until the next day to try again. The act of searching for the jiu-jitsu technique steps in our mind is what develops our recall. Not the number of times we repeat it after it has been found.

Memorizing a technique is a lot like planting a seed in the ground. At first you will have to water the seed on a frequent basis, but once it takes root it can water itself from the water underneath the surface of the soil. If you overwater the seed it will die, and if you do not water it enough it will die. Spaced repetition is how we provide the perfect amount of water to the seed of our memory. Once the short-term memory has taken root in our long-term memory, it will be able to take care of itself.

If you want to learn numerous jiu-jitsu techniques at the same time, like I did, you will want to use the *Leitner system*. The Leitner system is a popular method for efficiently using flash cards. It's named after the German scientist Sebastian Leitner. It's based on the concepts of spaced repetition, competency, and frequency intervals. The version of this method I prefer to use for jiu-jitsu techniques involves using three different note card boxes.

The first note card box has all the techniques that are new to me. These techniques require more than thirty seconds to recall. Regardless of the time, if I miss even one small step, the technique will automatically go into the first box. The first box holds the note cards of the techniques I will drill most often.

The second note card box has all the techniques that I can recite in under thirty seconds without any errors. This box houses the techniques that I still have to think about in order to recall. Even though I can recite these techniques without any errors, I'm still hesitant, and cannot fluently speak them yet. I will recite these techniques after the first box during every drill session.

The third and final note card box holds the techniques that I can instantly repeat without any hesitation. I will only recite these techniques once a week or in some cases once a month. If at any time I were to lose my fluency, I would immediately demote the technique back into the second or even the first box if I miss a step. Once I have proven to myself that I have regained fluency with the technique, I will promote it back to the third box. After you have a sufficient number of techniques in your third box, you will be ready to start the practice of visualization in the next chapter.

When we can quickly recite a jiu-jitsu technique on our first attempt every time we drill it, we will know that it is in our long-term memory. Fast recall speed is the primary indicator that a memory is coated with enough myelin. The thicker the myelin sheath is around a memory, the faster we can recall it. Your stopwatch will become the scientific instrument to measure both your progress and skill level.

In Summary:

1) Write the name of the technique on the blank side of a four-by-six-inch note card. Alternate pen colors for each letter and focus on your font and spacing.

2) Write your abbreviated notes at the top of the ruled side of the note card with a black pen.

3) Write your Fill In the Word technique letters under the abbreviated notes with a black pen.

4) Draw or write the names of your Fill In the Story technique pictures at the bottom of the note card with a red pen.

5) Divide your note cards into three boxes based on your ability to recall the technique.

CHAPTER 8

Ordinary Visualization

Ordinary visualization involves actively creating a mental picture of what we remember about a technique. Extraordinary visualization is passively watching the memory of the technique with a photographic memory. Since most of us were not born with a photographic memory, we will start by discussing the proper way to visualize jiu-jitsu techniques, using ordinary visualization. After we develop a strong foundation with ordinary visualization, we can explore the world of extraordinary visualization.

There are three stages of ordinary visualization that we will be using to mentally practice our techniques. The first stage involves recalling the technique name and visualizing the linking story that is associated with it. The second stage involves visualizing the technique with internal dialogue based on our abbreviated notes. The third and final stage involves mentally practicing the technique without a linking story or internal dialogue. After we can clearly visualize the technique in our mind, we will be ready to physically practice the technique in a future chapter.

Visualization will expose holes in your memory. You will need to fill in these holes by creating additional memories. The ability to clearly visualize your techniques relies on being able to remember as many small details about the technique as possible. The more you can remember about the technique the easier it will be to formulate a clear mental picture. For example, one step of a technique might involve grabbing the opponent's wrist. Instead of just visualizing yourself grabbing their wrist, notice how many fingers you use to complete the grab. What does their wrist feel like? Do they have a skinny wrist or is it wide and hard to hold? Is their wrist sweaty? Can you feel the tendons on their wrist? Can you feel their pulse? Notice how many questions I have about just one step. The more details we can observe, the higher the definition will be. Each detail is its own pixel. The more pixels we can add to our visualization the clearer it will become.

Once you have broken down the first step in as much detail as possible it's time to move on to the second step. You want to clearly see every aspect of the transition from one step to another. This is the mental glue that connects the two images. For example, the first step of the *trap and roll escape* involves grabbing the opponent's right wrist with my right hand. The second step involves grabbing the back of their right tricep with my left hand. I want to connect the visual of each step together by focusing on the movement of my body from one step to the next. This will provide a fluid visualization that requires less effort to observe. The questions I might ask myself are: Was it easy to grab the back of their tricep? Was my elbow bent as I grabbed their tricep? At what point did I turn my left wrist to grab the back of their tricep?

The beautiful thing about precisely detailing each movement is that we only have to do it a couple of times to get it to stick in our memory. We have already done most of the hard work in previous chapters. Now we get to start enjoying our spoils of war. It's time to start working with the mental products we have already created. When we memorized each step of a technique the visual in our mind was somewhat fragmented. Now we need to add additional photos to our visual to create a continuous picture. The more pictures we add, the more fluid the visualization will look.

When we watch a movie on television, we do not see thousands of individual frames. We only see the movie in one continuous loop. Low-resolution movies appear blurry and choppy compared to high-definition movies that are clear and fluid. The main difference between the two resolutions is the number of frames per second. In the film industry this is referred to as the *frame rate*. We can consider each frame to be one small movement of the technique. The key to creating a high-definition technique in our mind is to smoothly transition from one step to the next by adding as many frames as we can.

The next time you watch a movie, notice how many times it switches between camera angles. The movie goes in and out of different angles hundreds of times. This is how the director captivates your senses and keeps you watching. We must do the same thing with the motion pictures in our mind. We need to see the technique from multiple angles. Look at the technique from each side as well as from above. The more angles you can clearly visualize the technique from, the more captivating your visual will become. This will also help you when you try a technique from an angle you are not used to. If you have created thousands of angles in your mind, the technique should feel comfortable to you, regardless of the position you're in.

The act of visualizing our techniques from multiple angles is an aspect of *mental rotation*. Mental rotation is when the brain moves mental images around in order to understand what they are and where they belong in our mind. If the brain cannot locate where the mental image belongs, it engages our cognitive functions to find out. Mental rotation can be divided into five cognitive stages. The first stage consists of creating a mental image from all angles. The second stage rotates the mental image until a comparison can be made. The third stage makes a comparison between the angled image and the rotated image. The fourth stage decides if the two images are the same. The fifth and final stage reports the decision to our brain. This entire cognitive process takes place in a fraction of a second. When we hold the image of our jiu-jitsu technique in our mind for an extended period of time, we dramatically enhance this cognitive process. The more time we allow our brain to observe the technique from multiple angles in our mind, the better. **Ref. 99**

Numerous studies have demonstrated that musical skill, athletic performance, and fast reaction times are all closely associated with people who exhibit exceptional mental rotational abilities. In 2007, a study was published in the *Journal of Neuroscience* that supported this finding. Researchers discovered that musicians perform better on mental rotation tasks than non-musicians. They found that orchestra musicians' mental rotational task performance exhibited aptitude levels significantly higher than the average person. In 2012, a study was cited by the American Psychological Association that showed athletes and musicians with exceptional mental rotational skills had faster reaction times than the average person. **Ref. 100–101**

Another important aspect to consider when you are visualizing your techniques is your point of view. After you can see the technique from different angles in the second person, you will need to transition into viewing the technique in the first person. In the film industry they call this a *point-of-view shot*. The difference between watching a movie with a virtual reality headset and watching it without one is dramatic. The first-person view that you receive from watching with virtual reality activates biochemical responses in your body that are similar to real life. A first-person view engages your senses in a way that second-person viewing cannot. **Ref. 93**

You can watch jiu-jitsu training videos all day long, but you do not get a first-person view until you mentally perform the technique yourself. Watching videos helped us to memorize the steps but now it's time to get ready to perform the technique. If you are having a hard time visualizing the technique from a first-person view, you can practice the technique with a dummy or training partner. This will help create the memories needed to visualize the technique from a first-person view.

In addition to visualizing in the first person, you will also want to change virtual training partners on a regular basis. Have your virtual opponent try different things as you are completing the technique in your mind. This visualization exercise will stay with you long after you master the technique. If you have ambitions of competing in the sport of jiu-jitsu, visualizing your opponent ahead of time can help prepare you for the real match.

Olympians use visualization on a daily basis to improve their skills. When you have defeated the opponent in your mind, the job is already half done. After you can clearly visualize yourself performing a new technique with virtual opponents, you will be ready to develop the neural connections from your brain to your muscles. For now, let's take a closer look at the three stages of ordinary visualization.

First Stage:

The first stage of visualization involves recalling the technique name and visualizing the linking story that is associated with it. Now that you have graduated to the visualization stage, you will not be able to rely on your note cards any longer. You will need to recall your techniques from memory based on your mind map. The visuals you have associated with the technique names will also give you the first visual of the linking story. You will need to visualize the technique in the first person as the story tells it. For example, if you are visualizing the *trap and roll escape*, your hands will need to be in the shape of bear traps, and so on. After you can clearly visualize the linking stories that are associated with all your technique names, you will be ready for stage two.

Second Stage:

The second stage of visualization involves visualizing the technique with internal dialogue based on your abbreviated notes. For this stage of visualization, you will recall just the name of the technique and not the linking story. At this point in your memory development, you should no longer be relying on associating pictures with your technique names. You should immediately know what the name of the technique is based on its location in your mind map. Now you can simply recall the technique name and immediately start reciting its steps.

The main difference between memory recall and visualization is that you are going to act out the steps in your mind as you mentally recite the steps. This stage of visualization is very powerful. You will start to become your own instructor who barks out orders for your virtual self to complete. Variations of this practice can lead to an increase in self-discipline. Once your mind and body figure out that your internal voice is their leader, they will assume a subordinate role and obey. This is when sheep become shepherds.

Third Stage:

The third and final stage of visualization involves mentally practicing the technique without a linking story or internal dialogue. This stage is perhaps the most relaxing because it requires the least amount of mental effort. Now you recall the technique name and immediately visualize yourself in the first person performing the technique. If at any point the visualization becomes fragmented, you will need to add additional details. The goal of this stage is to effortlessly visualize the technique. If you are still struggling to recall the steps in high definition, slow down and take your time. The memory of this technique is going to be with you for the rest of your life. The mental effort you exert today will lead to the clarity you enjoy tomorrow. If your visualizations become clear enough, they can evolve into what people refer to as photographic memories. This will be covered in the next chapter.

In Summary:

1) Recall the pictures that spell out the technique name and visualize the linking story that is associated with them.

2) Visualize the technique in the first person as the story tells it.

3) Then recall the technique name without pictures, and mentally recite the steps in the technique as you visualize yourself performing it.

4) Finish by visualizing yourself performing the technique without linking stories or internal commentary.

CHAPTER 9

Extraordinary Visualization

Now that you have some experience with ordinary visualization, it's time to look at extraordinary visualization. Nikola Tesla was a renowned inventor and engineer, known for his exceptional visualization skills. His ability to mentally conceive and manipulate complex inventions was a key factor in his groundbreaking discoveries. In order for us to develop similar visualization skills, we need to take a closer look at how he was able to accomplish such mental feats.

Tesla possessed a photographic memory, allowing him to recall intricate details of diagrams, designs, and scientific principles. His photographic memory enabled him to mentally visualize and manipulate complex electrical circuits without the need for physical drawings or calculations. Photographic memory is also known as eidetic memory. It refers to the mental faculty of recalling vivid images, sounds, or other sensory information in high definition. People with a photographic memory can mentally recreate and retain visual information in a manner similar to viewing a physical photograph or video.

While some people claim to have a photographic memory, scientific research suggests that true photographic memory is extremely rare. I was able to develop a limited form of photographic memory as a result of intense visualization training. I was not born with this ability, so I know from firsthand experience that it can be cultivated. The more I practiced visualizing in the ordinary way, the more photographic and extraordinary my visualizations became. By photographic, I'm referring to lifelike visuals in my mind that are similar to watching a movie on a screen. Photographic mental images have a life of their own, in the same way we cannot control the next scene of a movie that we are watching.

With ordinary visualization, we have to consciously recall the memory of the image. Then we control what aspects of the memory we want to observe based on our intention. With ordinary visualization, our conscious awareness takes on the shape of the memory itself. Jiddu Krishnamurti referred to this as "*the observer is the observed.*" Krishnamurti was a speaker who played a key role in Bruce Lee's philosophical development.

With a photographic memory, our conscious awareness is separate from the memory. Photographic memories appear in our mind as if they were physical scenes. The best way to understand what a photographic image looks like is to print out a solid red triangle that is about three inches in size. Now hold that picture about two feet in front of your eyes. Stare at the image for as long as you can without blinking. After you're forced to blink, close your eyes and passively observe the afterimage of the triangle. You will notice that you do not have to exert any effort to see the afterimage. The triangle appears of its own accord in a green color that is the inverse color of red. Stare at the afterimage until it slowly fades away. Even though you are just observing an afterimage that was burned into your retina, this is nearly identical to how it will look if you develop a photographic memory. The image appears on its own without any conscious effort on your behalf.

To prove that the afterimage is created from your retina and not in the visual cortex of your brain, you can close one eye and stare at the red triangle. Then open your closed eye and close your eye that was staring at the red triangle. You will notice that an afterimage only appears on the eye that was staring at the object. If the afterimage appeared in both eyes, you would know that the afterimage had been consolidated in the visual cortex.

Another afterimage experiment you can conduct will involve closing your eyes in a dark room. When you close your eyes in a dark room for a minimum of ten minutes, your eyes will become approximately ten thousand times more sensitive to light. It's caused by the chemical rhodopsin in the rods of your retina. Rhodopsin is a light-sensitive chemical composed of retinal and opsin. Retinal is a derivative of vitamin A and opsin is a protein. From the moment your eyes stop receiving light from an external source your rhodopsin levels start to increase. **Ref. 95**

We will use the increased presence of rhodopsin in your retina to create an afterimage of an entire scene. To conduct this experiment, cover your eyes or wear an eye mask for at least ten minutes to allow them to adapt to the dark. Now open your eyes and look at a scene in front of you for one second, then quickly close your eyes again. You should see a faint picture of the entire scene in purple and black. After a period of time, the image will reverse to black and purple. The purple color you will see in the afterimage is the rhodopsin. That's why rhodopsin is often called *the purple chemical*.

Once you start to observe your jiu-jitsu techniques passively like the triangle, or purple scene afterimage, you will know that you have started to develop a photographic memory. You don't need to have a photographic memory to succeed in visualizing techniques. An ordinary visualization session will be more than enough to rehearse jiu-jitsu techniques in your mind. The average person will not become passive enough to watch photographic images in their mind. They are instinctively afraid that this will result in psychosis or schizophrenia. This instinctive fear is an aspect of our ego that suppresses painful memories. The problem with this vestigial fear is that it also blocks the flow of photographic memories. Some readers will be able to overcome this primal fear quicker than others, and many never will. The smaller a person's ego is, the easier it will be to overcome this habitual fear reflex.

I must admit that I was scared of photographic images when they first started to surface. My fear of them caused the neural wormhole to instinctively close. It took several months to be able to get the photographic images to flow again. I feared that I would lose control of my mind if I let the images flow unchecked. In the beginning, we have to let the images flow of their own accord without willfully directing them. Once we develop the skill of passively observing the photographic images, we can start to direct them toward one subject, like jiu-jitsu.

Most people associate their entire identity with their memories. If our memories start to play on their own, outside of our conscious control, it's easy to see how we could feel we are losing control of ourselves. The key to developing a photographic memory is the ability to separate memories from our true self. If you think about it deeply enough, you will discover that we are not our memories. We are the sentient being that is aware of our memories. Our memories are nothing more than mental records of the past or imaginary projections of the future. Becoming aware of this fact will help you to observe your memories as a passive observer, and not a reactive participant.

The left side of our brain wants to control every aspect of our thoughts and the right side of our brain wants to passively daydream about them. The secret is to observe both aspects of our mind without a preference toward one side. Then we can start to develop the corpus callosum at the center of our brain, rather than one side over the other. True creativity finds itself in the flow of balance. When our conscious awareness looks at both sides of our mind with equal attention, we have a decent shot at joining the ranks of Albert Einstein, Nikola Tesla, Leonardo Davinci, and many other creative geniuses.

In order to consciously observe both sides of our mind, we need to connect the left brain to the right brain through a neural wormhole that goes through the corpus callosum. Every jiu-jitsu technique you have ever watched is stored in your right brain in its entirety. The problem is we need to consciously access this video so that we can watch it in our mind. This is a lot like looking through a peephole. You set the intention to see a specific technique and then you look through that peephole to watch it play. Intention delivered the video to the hole you have drilled through the corpus callosum. This was an action that required mental effort. Then you get to passively watch the video now that it has been delivered to your peephole.

As you observe the desired technique in the peephole, it's nearly identical to watching it in virtual reality. That's why it's so important to visualize your techniques in the first person during ordinary visualization sessions. We want to see our techniques through the peephole in the first person, because if it appears in the second person, you would be better off just watching the technique on your television. If extraordinary visualization does not have a practical application, you are just playing mind games.

When you create a conscious opening in your right brain, it's considered the first step of internal martial arts. Ancient martial artists called this *punching through,* and yogis call it *opening the third eye.* Ordinary visualization uses force/activity and extraordinary visualization uses anti-force/passivity. Yang is martial activity and yin is artistic passivity. When the two are perfectly balanced you get a true martial artist that is expressed with the yin-yang symbol. Each dot on the opposite side of the symbol represents a neural wormhole. Observing the dark within light and the light within dark. This is the harmony of opposites.

Throughout history there have been savants who have been able to consciously access the right side of their brain. The problem with many of these savants is that they are unable to sustain attention in their left brain long enough to interact with society in a normal way. Kim Peek was a savant who could read two pages of a book at a time and recall nearly every detail of every book he had ever read. His left eye would read the left page as his right eye read the right page. He could read an entire book in a matter of minutes and quote every word verbatim. According to an article in *The Times* newspaper, he could accurately recall the contents of over twelve thousand books. Peek's brain was studied by some of the best researchers in modern neuroscience. It was discovered that he had agenesis of the corpus callosum. ACC is a rare birth defect in which there is a complete or partial absence of the corpus callosum. Researchers speculate that his brain developed unusual neural connections between the left and right hemisphere that resulted in his extraordinary memory skills. **Ref. 102**

If we were to have unfiltered access to our right brain at all times, we would experience sensory overload. The left brain is what helps to keep things in check and allows us to follow civilized laws and behaviors. By creating only one small neural wormhole, we are able to interact with our right brain without it taking over. This allows us to function in society but still reap the benefits of interacting directly with our right brain. Albert Einstein's brain was one of the best examples of consciously connecting the left and right hemisphere together in a controlled way. **Ref. 9**

Without light we cannot have darkness and vice versa. The left part of our brain can be considered light, and the right side can be considered darkness. The key is to drill a small neural wormhole into our dark right brain so that we can see it with the light of our conscious awareness. When we dream, we are at the mercy of whatever happens in our right brain. When we are awake, we get to consciously make choices as to what we want to have happen using our left brain. The key is to get the best of both worlds by only consciously accessing a small part of our subconscious right brain at a time.

When we are done peeping through our neural wormhole, we need to intentionally close the door on the hole. If we do not set the intention to close the hole, we could experience an unwanted flow of photographic images from the right side of our brain during our daily activities. This could possibly lead to psychosis if it was left unchecked. The key is to control the access port to our right brain so that we do not get lost in a reverie of daydreams while we are awake in our daily lives. This process happens naturally when we wake up from a dream. If you find that you wake up in the morning and you're still in a sleep like state known as a trance, you will know that the neural wormhole did not properly close.

The neural wormhole is located on the backside of your forehead. Photographic images will appear on the void mental screen behind your forehead. It's the same screen that the afterimages appear on. Yogis refer to this space as the chidakasha. When you are ready to close the neural wormhole, you will need to roll an imaginary boulder across the entire backside of your forehead. This sets a clear intention to block incoming photographic images. When we combine our intention from the left brain with our imagination from the right brain, magic happens.

Now that I have described my theory of consciously connecting the left brain to the right brain through a neural wormhole in the corpus callosum. It's time to see if you can substantiate this theory and make it a fact for yourself. In previous chapters, I cited scientific references to help validate my statements, but now we are approaching a subject matter that can only be validated by your own personal experiences.

It's important to keep in mind that a photographic memory is still a controversial subject in scientific circles. Some researchers believe it exists and others are still skeptical because they have never experienced it for themselves. The only reason we can practically approach the subject matter is because your jiu-jitsu visualizations may become so intense that they take on a life of their own. I had serious reservations about discussing the topic of photographic memories in this book. It would have been much easier to stick with just ordinary visualization because it's a universal practice that everyone can do. The only reason I decided to discuss photographic memories is because you may be one of the rare people who can observe them in your mind. I would rather run the risk of sounding unfounded than have you observe a photographic image for the first time and not know what it is.

As someone who can see photographic images, I know firsthand that the images I observe in my mind are very similar to the afterimages we all see after staring at an object. This should give you some reassurance when you first start to see your own visualizations come to life. In the beginning all you will be able to see are ordinary mental images, but with time and tenacity you will hopefully start to see extraordinary mental images.

Many researchers call a photographic memory an eidetic memory without clearly discerning the difference. From my own personal experience an eidetic memory precedes a photographic memory. With an eidetic memory a person can look at a picture for only a couple of seconds and the image is burned into their retina with such clarity that they can recall this image for up to five minutes. By this definition an afterimage is nothing more than an eidetic memory. For me the main difference between an eidetic memory and a photographic memory is that a photographic memory can be summoned by my intention any time I want to see it. That means it's not just a temporary phenomenon caused by the retina.

Out of all the books I have read in my life, none of them have been able to accurately explain what a photographic memory is, much less provide a method to develop it. The closest I have ever come to finding books on this subject matter has come from books on advanced yogic mind practices. One such practice that is rumored to develop a photographic memory is called *trataka*. The word *trataka* is Sanskrit, meaning to "look" or "gaze." The *Haṭha Yoga Pradīpikā* defines trataka as "Looking intently with an unwavering gaze at a small point until tears are shed." The *Haṭha Yoga Pradīpikā* is a classic fifteenth-century Sanskrit yoga manual written by Svātmārāma.

The traditional practice of trataka involves staring at a candle flame until your eyes tear up. You then close your eyes and passively stare at the afterimage of the flame until it fades away. With practice the afterimage will stay in your field of awareness for longer periods of time. Eventually the afterimage of the flame can be summoned at will any time you want to see it. This would be the graduation from an eidetic memory to a true photographic memory.

It's worth noting that Nikola Tesla had a close friendship with a yogi by the name of Swami Vivekananda. Vivekananda was widely recognized as a leading expert on photographic memory. He allegedly memorized a seven-hundred-page book in one hour to demonstrate the power of his photographic memory. The main difference between yogi Vivekananda, and the savant Kim Peek, was that Vivekananda did not have any brain abnormalities. Vivekananda gave credit to yoga practices for his extraordinary memory skills. **Ref. 94**

I do not currently possess Kim Peek's or Swami Vivekananda's degree of memory skill, so I do not claim to be a savant, or a yogi. The only photographic memories that I'm currently interested in observing are the jiu-jitsu techniques that I have spent the most time visualizing. I prefer to keep my scope of internal observation focused on practical applications, rather than getting caught up in unproductive imaginings.

One of the side effects of intense mental concentration is a heightened degree of sensitivity to our internal thoughts. If this is something that disturbs you, back off your visualization training for a while and see if the heightened sensitivity goes away. It's impossible to develop a high-powered brain without becoming aware of our internal mindscape. This form of metacognition can serve as a valuable tool if you are interested in personal growth through self-exploration. The maxim "know thyself" will take on an entirely new meaning for someone who becomes self-aware.

Once you are able to clearly visualize your jiu-jitsu techniques internally, you will need to externally express your internal skill. The first level of expressing your internal skill involves developing muscle memory. This will be covered in the next chapter. The second level of expressing your internal skill involves implementing strategies. This will be covered in the final chapter. The third level of expressing your internal skill exceeds the scope of this book. In the future, I may choose to share some of the higher internal skills for those who are interested.

In Summary:

1) Develop a photographic memory by visualizing your jiu-jitsu techniques every day with as much clarity as possible.

2) Add small details to your techniques every time you visualize them to increase the odds of *punching through* the corpus callosum.

3) Passively observe the subconscious images that flow into your awareness without judging or reacting to them.

4) After you become passive enough to observe subconscious images, develop the intention to see a specific jiu-jitsu technique in the first person on your mind screen.

5) Always finish your visualization practice by intentionally rolling a large boulder in front of the neural wormhole. When you are ready for the next visualization session, mentally roll the boulder out of the way.

CHAPTER 10

Muscle Memory

Before we address the practical application of developing neural connections from our brain to our muscles, we need to explore the scientific principles that support it. Muscle memory is a phenomenon that has fascinated researchers, athletes, musicians, and learners of various skills for hundreds of years. It's the magical ability of our muscles to perform actions without conscious effort, as if they have memorized the movements themselves. From playing a sport to perfecting a jiu-jitsu technique, muscle memory plays a pivotal role in achieving excellence. This chapter delves into the mechanisms of muscle memory as well as methods to develop it.

Mechanisms of Muscle Memory

At its core, muscle memory is not actually stored in the muscles themselves, but rather within the intricate network of the brain. This process involves the coordination of various parts of the nervous system, from sensory receptors in the muscles to the cerebral cortex in the brain. The key to muscle memory lies in the brain's ability to optimize the neural pathways associated with a particular action.

The brain's remarkable ability to reorganize its neural pathways is known as *neuroplasticity*. Neuroplasticity is the cornerstone of muscle memory. As we repeatedly perform a specific action, the brain refines the communication between neurons responsible for that action. This leads to more efficient and coordinated signals, resulting in improved performance over time.

The human brain, often hailed as the most complex and adaptable organ in the body, possesses a remarkable capacity to change its organization and structure. This phenomenon challenges the traditional notion of a fixed and unchanging brain structure. Neuroplasticity underscores the brain's ability to reorganize, adapt, and remodel its neural pathways in response to experience, learning, injury, and even environmental changes.

The main aspect of neuroplasticity is its reliance on experience. The brain's ability to rewire itself is most evident during learning and skill acquisition. This experience-dependent plasticity is particularly prominent in early life, but it persists throughout adulthood, albeit to a slightly lesser degree. When we learn a jiu-jitsu technique, the brain adjusts its neural pathways to accommodate the new skill. After the new pathways are established, they are coated in myelin to speed up transmission and prevent neural misfires. **Ref. 1**

Learning a new jiu-jitsu technique also involves creating and strengthening specific connections between relevant neurons. Neurons communicate at synapses, where the strength of the connection between two neurons determines the efficiency of the signal transmission. With each repetition of a movement, the synapses involved in that action become stronger, and the neural pathways leading to the synapses become thicker due to myelination. This results in a faster, smoother, and overall more efficient action potential. The more fluid a movement becomes, the less conscious effort is required. Conscious effort drains our energy rapidly. That is why a white belt in jiu-jitsu uses a lot more energy than a black belt. The white belt has to deliberately move their muscles, whereas a black belt automatically moves them.

In addition to experience, studies have shown that exposing individuals to enriched and stimulating environments can also enhance neuroplasticity. Environments that offer a variety of sensory experiences and cognitive challenges encourage the growth of new neural connections. This fact should help jiu-jitsu teachers structure their classes in ways that are not static and boring. The more stimulating a training session is, the easier it will be to perfect the techniques being taught. **Ref. 103**

There are three main brain regions involved with developing muscle memory. The basal ganglia and cerebellum are parts of our brain that are heavily involved in the formation and execution of motor skills. The basal ganglia refines movements based on feedback and reward, while the cerebellum aids in balance, coordination, and precision. These brain regions work in concert with the cerebral cortex to establish the neural pathways responsible for muscle memory.

The acquisition of muscle memory is deeply intertwined with the learning process. Whether we are learning to ride a bike or mastering a complex jiu-jitsu technique, several stages characterize the journey toward ingrained proficiency. In the initial phase, the practitioner consciously analyzes the technique, breaking it down into smaller components. Mistakes are frequent, and the process can be mentally taxing. However, this stage is crucial for understanding the fundamental aspects of the technique.

As practice continues, the student's performance improves, and the focus shifts from conscious analysis to refining the execution. Errors become less frequent, and the movements start to feel more fluid. This is the stage where muscle memory begins to take root. With consistent and deliberate practice, the skill eventually becomes automatic. Muscle memory dominates this stage of development, enabling the student to perform the jiu-jitsu technique without consciously thinking about each step. At this point, techniques are executed effortlessly, and the practitioner can focus on other elements, such as strategy.

This is why we start by memorizing a technique, then we follow up with visualization, muscle memory, and ultimately strategy. Every aspect of visual jiu-jitsu builds upon the previous step. When the formula is followed with precision, we can master a new technique in a very short period of time. Now that you have a better understanding of the neurological mechanisms involved with muscle memory, we can start to implement methods to develop it.

Developing Muscle Memory

A good analogy to describe the development of muscle memory comes from a scene in *The Karate Kid* where Daniel spends days waxing Mr. Miyagi's cars and staining his fence. When Daniel grows frustrated from not being taught karate, he wants to give up. Mr. Miyagi then shows him how the movements of waxing the cars and staining the fence developed the muscle memory necessary for performing actions automatically in response to an attack. Although this is just a movie, the principles being taught are very real.

The first step in developing muscle memory requires slow and precise repetitions to activate neuroplasticity and myelination. If we perform the same action slightly differently each time, we will create multiple neural pathways that are all competing to execute the same action potential. This will create inconsistencies in your performance due to neuronal misfires. If you verbally or mentally coach yourself through each step of the technique, you will be less likely to make mistakes. This simple fact is what separates a neophyte from a master. This is also the biggest error I have observed in jiu-jitsu.

The traditional way jiu-jitsu has been taught in the past involves the instructor demonstrating the technique, followed by the student replicating their movements. Obviously, there is nothing wrong with this approach because it has produced a lot of highly skilled martial artists. Unfortunately, this is not the most efficient way to develop muscle memory. When you practice a technique with a training partner before you have properly developed muscle memory solo, you will be hardwiring several competing neural pathways. This is because every training partner is different. The differences in body type and skill between opponents will require your body to move differently in order to accommodate their movements. This will often result in what is referred to as *negative training*.

Negative training is when you create bad habits as a result of not executing proper technique. If the body has been properly wired to perform a technique with precision, it will automatically adjust to different body types. The problem occurs when the body is thrown into the fire without having first developed a healthy neural pathway through slow and precise movements. One of the best practices I have witnessed concerning proper muscle memory development has come from watching karate masters practice what are known as *katas*.

A kata is a precise sequence of movements that are focused solely on executing proper technique. You do not practice katas with a training partner in the beginning for the reasons I have already mentioned. The goal of katas is to develop muscle memory so that the technique can be performed automatically in a real fight. Each kata represents one technique. The more techniques you have, the more katas you will need to practice. In jiu-jitsu we refer to this as a *drill* instead of calling it a *kata*. The importance of drilling techniques cannot be understated. If done correctly, you will properly develop the neural pathways needed to perform a technique without consciously thinking about it. You will also maintain the myelin sheath around the pathways if you practice drills on a regular basis.

One of the first jiu-jitsu masters I observed with fully developed neural pathways was Rickson Gracie. He had the ability to go on mental autopilot and defeat his opponents without thinking. This is a very high degree of mastery, and it symbolizes the graduation of the muscle memory stage. Another jiu-jitsu master who has a similar level of development is a practitioner by the name of Mikey Musumeci. Mikey has stated that he *blacks out* in the heat of a fight. He has described his blackouts as a brief period of time during a match when he subconsciously performs the techniques without thought or conscious perception. He noticed that when he performs his techniques perfectly, he is not conscious of his movements. His blackouts signify a high degree of muscle memory development. It's worth noting that Mikey is known for his obsession with drilling techniques for several hours each day.

In a book titled *The Talent Code* written by Daniel Coyle, the author outlines three main elements that he discovered when investigating some of the most talented athletes and musicians around the world. If you have not read his book, I strongly recommend that you do. It will validate many of the lessons you have learned in this book. The first element he discovered among all the elite athletes and musicians he interviewed was that they all participated in *deep practice*. Deep practice is defined as repetitive practice of small movements that lead to perfection of the whole movement.

Coyle discovered that most of the elite athletes he investigated broke their skills down into smaller parts called chunks. You already know how powerful chunking is for memory but now you will discover how important it is for performance. The author discovered chunking when he visited an elite music school in New York. He noticed that their sheet music was chopped up so that a piece of music would first be practiced in random order. When the musicians finally played the whole piece, they had a much deeper understanding of every element or chunk. This would be the equivalent of learning how to grab an opponent's wrist, then how to trap their leg, and eventually how to bridge and roll the opponent over to escape from the bottom of mount. Can you imagine how good you would become at grabbing a person's wrist if that's the only thing you practiced for a week straight? The dividing line between mediocrity and excellence is wide.

Another element Coyle discovered among elite athletes and musicians was that their coaches allowed them to learn from their mistakes instead of correcting their mistakes for them. Elite jiu-jitsu coaches such as John Danaher have been using this element of self-correction for years. He may ask one of his athletes why they are doing something a particular way, but he seems to prefer that they figure it out for themselves. John defines this in his instructional videos as *heuristic learning*. I refer to this as *autodidactic learning*, which is a more intense level of self-education on the learning scale.

The third element that Coyle discovered about deep practice was that nearly all the athletes and musicians he researched were constantly challenging their limits. Once a skill had been mastered, they were expected to make the skill harder. This was the secret to keeping the myelin growing around their neural pathways. The moment the elite athletes stopped pushing their limits they started to decline in skill. This is attributed to complacency caused by what we perceive to be mastery.

If we think we have mastered something, we lose interest in it and want to move on to the next conquest. The jiu-jitsu masters of today will look like white belts compared to practitioners in the future. If you spar with white belts, it will be challenging when you spar with black belts. The key is to constantly challenge your skills and learn from your mistakes. This self-correcting element is shared by nearly all elite athletes. If your ego does not like to be challenged, you will remain among the ranks of mediocrity.

As a novice to jiu-jitsu, I'm not qualified to offer you specific advice on sparring with training partners. This should be left in the hands of black belts who have earned the right to be called masters. They can offer you constructive feedback based on their years of experience. Your job is to learn their techniques and their job is to make sure you practice them correctly. Thankfully, there are many highly qualified instructors located throughout the world.

Once you graduate from the muscle memory stage, you will be ready to enter the realm of strategizing your moves. This will allow you to always be several steps ahead of your opponent. Before a person can play chess, they must first know the moves. When they know the moves, they can start memorizing strategies. The lessons you will learn from the

Grandmasters of chess in the next chapter will help you reach levels in jiu-jitsu that are currently unheard of. Now that you have mastered the techniques of jiu-jitsu, it's time to learn how to win.

In Summary:

1) Verbally or mentally direct your body to perform each step of the technique from memory. You need to become your own jiu-jitsu coach.

2) Drill one small movement in a technique by yourself until you can easily perform it. Then move on to the next small movement until you eventually perform the entire technique with ease. A grappling dummy can also be used at this stage of development.

3) Once you can automatically perform the technique by yourself, start to drill the technique with a willing training partner. Take turns from each position and make sure both parties are compliant without resistance.

4) After you can perform the technique with perfect form, start to add resistance. Have your training partner slowly increase their intensity. If your technique starts to get sloppy, slow down and focus on proper form.

5) After every sparring session, finish by slowing down and cleaning up your technique. A fight requires flexibility, but you should always return to your original kata. Train clean so that you can fight dirty.

6) Learn from your mistakes. Figure out why the technique is not working and make the necessary adjustments. Rely on your own self to solve the problem but be grateful for the constructive advice your experienced instructor has to offer.

7) Challenge yourself by training with opponents of a higher skill level. Neutralize your ego and accept the reality of your current skill set. If you cannot acknowledge your current limits, you will never be able to overcome them. If you currently get tapped twenty times during a training session, focus on only getting tapped nineteen times the next time you train. Small victories will eventually lead to big victories.

CHAPTER 11

Memorizing Strategies

The game of chess is often split into two elements. One part is concerned with tactics and the other part is concerned with strategies. Tactics are to chess what techniques are to jiu-jitsu. The number of similarities you will see between chess and jiu-jitsu is striking. For now, I'm going to discuss the differences between tactics and strategy in chess. You may find that it sounds like I'm talking about jiu-jitsu, but I assure you these are chess ideologies.

Chess tactics are mostly known as a forceful combination of moves that claim one of your opponent's pieces or lead to checkmate. Such decisive tactics usually become possible because of an oversight by either of the players. Chess strategy, on the other hand, refers to the long-term objectives you want to achieve. In other words, strategy requires planning, but tactics require execution. Strategy is the intended plan of action, but tactics are the reactions we have to what we are observing.

For example, I plan on submitting my opponent with a rear naked choke, but they roll over to their side. Now instead of choking them, I submit them with an armlock. My strategy was one thing, but my tactic was something else. If the opponent had stayed on their stomach, I would have finished with a rear naked choke. What we plan to do and what we actually do is determined by what we observe our opponent doing.

At first glance you may wonder why we should intentionally strategize if we are forced to execute a reactional tactic to win 99 percent of the time. Even though tactics and strategy are not the same thing, they work in unison in that tactics are often used to achieve strategic objectives. For example, my strategy is to ultimately submit my opponent by rear naked choke. In order to do this, I need to be in the back mount position. If I'm currently in the top mount position, I need to get them to roll over. To achieve this objective, I initiate a twisting arm control position, or a *gift wrap* as it is sometimes called. My strategy is to get the opponent to roll over, but if they do not roll over, I will initiate an armlock. If I were to win by armlock this would be considered a tactical victory. If the opponent had rolled over and I finished them with a rear naked choke, this would be considered a strategic victory. Both moves shared the same objective, which was to win.

This concept of strategy versus tactics is extremely important for jiu-jitsu practitioners to understand. This one concept will elevate the art and sport of jiu-jitsu to levels we currently could not even imagine. Right now, most practitioners, even at the highest levels of jiu-jitsu rely mostly on tactics rather than strategy. If the opponent does this, I do that, and so on. Even the elite jiu-jitsu players who are capable of planning a couple of steps ahead are nowhere near world-class chess players. The difference between being two steps ahead of your opponent and ten steps ahead of them is drastic.

Novice chess players are instructed to stick with the principle moves in the beginning just like jiu-jitsu practitioners.

They are also coached to accumulate small advantages by improving their position in a slow, progressive manner. At this level of their development the closest they come to a strategy is to execute a short combination of moves that improves their position in some way. In jiu-jitsu this is commonly referred to as *position before submission*. If world-class chess players were not so mentally ahead of jiu-jitsu practitioners, you would think that chess players were stealing their knowledge from jiu-jitsu.

With chess you must focus on legal moves. In jiu-jitsu you get to cheat if you are bigger and stronger than your opponent. You cannot forcibly push an opponent's chess piece off the table because you are stronger than them. Chess relies solely on memory of the moves and strategy. Jiu-jitsu relies primarily on memory of the moves and force. This is why world-class chess players are so far ahead of jiu-jitsu practitioners. When jiu-jitsu catches up to chess, we will see it dominate mixed martial arts competitions once again.

Chess players often put a lot of pressure on themselves to find a winning move in every position. Most of the time such a move doesn't exist. In most positions you are simply looking for a way to improve your position or prevent your opponent from improving theirs. Sound familiar? This is one of the basic principles of jiu-jitsu. In chess, players will develop an entire strategy just to improve a position. Then they will have another strategy to prevent their opponent from improving theirs. After the first two objectives have been secured, they go in for the kill and claim one of their opponent's pieces. They will move through the entire chess board one piece at a time until they reach checkmate.

This means one game of chess involves numerous strategies to reach the ultimate goal of checkmate. For those who are not familiar with chess, there are sixteen total pieces on each side to start with. The goal is to trap your opponent's king by preventing him from being able to move. Once their king can no longer move this is called checkmate and you win. In jiu-jitsu this would be called a pin and not a submission. In chess you cannot actually capture the king, you can only trap him. If you could capture the king, it would be considered a submission in jiu-jitsu.

It's very hard to compete against someone who has a plan for a plan. In jiu-jitsu the first strategy is to secure a dominant position. Then to maintain the dominant position so that we can prevent the opponent from executing their strategy. Then we can start to work on a submission. In chess this is called *action, prevention, and obliteration.* Many world-class jiu-jitsu practitioners talk about having a small number of techniques but a large number of variations. This means they have a limited number of moves, but an unlimited number of ways to execute them.

A better way to look at a jiu-jitsu strategy would be to say that our end goal is to finish the opponent with an armlock. In order to do this, we need a strategy to get the opponent down to the ground and secure a dominant position. Once we have the dominant position, we need to exhaust the opponent by preventing their escape. This is technically checkmate in a real street fight. Once we have maintained the dominant position long enough, we finish with the armlock.

This one goal required numerous strategies. If we had tried to go straight for the armlock the opponent would have laughed at us. If you're not in a position to get a submission it's not going to happen. Even throwing a punch or kick requires proper position before you can execute the strike. If you throw a punch at an opponent from ten feet away, you're going to miss. Chess players rely on position over everything else. It's position that creates checkmate, not the number of pieces you claim along the way.

If you learn anything from this chapter, I hope it's the fact that position should always be your first objective in jiu-jitsu. If you control the position, you control the fight. In the beginning your sole focus should be on creating strategies to secure superior positions. Remember, a strategy is preplanned, and tactics are used in reaction to moves that are not planned. It's easy to get sidetracked when an opponent blocks one of the steps in your strategy. The key is to use tactics to get back into a position to re-execute your strategy.

Gordan Ryan is famous for announcing the submission he will win with before he fights because he has mastered the art of strategy. Regardless of the tactics he uses to execute his strategy he finds a way to finish the fight with a predetermined submission. Grandmasters of chess will also demonstrate similar feats of mental fortitude. They can truly play with their opponent's minds because their strategy and tactics are on a more advanced level.

Many chess players subscribe to the theory that chess is 99 percent tactics. And while this may be true in terms of the raw moves that are made, you do not simply stumble upon the correct position in which to deploy all those tactics you worked so hard to memorize. Instead, you rely upon strategy to help you set those tactics up and steer your opponent in the direction you want them to go so that you can employ your tactics. Bobby Fischer was a Grandmaster of chess and one of the best players of the twenty-first century. When he was asked to divulge his secret to playing chess so well, he said: *"Tactics flow from a superior position."*

Chess players are masters at luring opponents into a position that they already have the blocks and traps set for. They will intentionally give their opponent a move to sucker them into a prearranged trap that they have memorized. This is a clever form of intentional persuasion. World-class chess players and stage magicians are masters at persuasion. When you are planning a move ten steps ahead with numerous routes and variations to account for all the different decisions your opponent can make, it will be very hard for them to defeat you. **Ref. 104**

One of the secrets Grandmasters of chess keep close to their chest is the art of illusion. Stage magicians have been stunning audiences for generations with their sleight of hand tricks. The main goal of stage magic is to divert your senses so that you do not see what they are truly doing. When you are captivated by the coin in the magician's right hand you do not see the coin they are palming in their left hand. When they magically cause one coin to turn into two coins our senses are amazed. The art of illusion is usually only practiced at the highest levels of chess. I have yet to see anyone in jiu-jitsu use it consistently to a high degree.

The effectiveness of our strategy relies on our ability to control our opponent's reactions. If the opponent knows what our next move is, they will be able to counter it. We use this fact to intentionally disguise our true motives. The better we become at hiding our strategy, the more effective it will become. The ability to mislead our opponent's reactions is the key to executing our game plan. For example, if I need the opponent to roll over to their stomach, I will punch them in the face until they roll over.

They will think my goal is to punch them in the face but it's actually just to get them to roll over. As soon as they roll over,

I will pretend I want to twist their arm behind their back. When they focus on defending their arm, I will wrap my arm around their neck and finish with a rear naked choke. This was my strategy all along, but my opponent thought I wanted to punch them in the face. Then they thought I wanted to break their arm. It probably came as a surprise when I wrapped my arm around their neck.

My strategy was to finish the fight with a rear naked choke, but I used the tactics of striking and an armlock to execute the strategy. At any point along the way the opponent could have given up. Maybe they did not like the fact that I had them pinned. They could have given up before I even threw a punch. There were numerous outs along the way for the opponent to give up. That's why most jiu-jitsu practitioners put so much emphasis on techniques over strategy. Most fights are won before you finish executing the strategy. This may work on less-skilled opponents, but it will not always work with those who have a similar skill set. That's why there are so many stalemates in the sport of jiu-jitsu.

One of the best methods I have worked with to develop an effective strategy is to create a flowchart. A flowchart is a visual representation of the jiu-jitsu techniques we have to choose from in order to complete our strategy. For example, we start with one strategy, which is to submit our opponent with a rear naked choke. The first technique on our flowchart will be a single leg takedown. The second technique will be establishing the back mount. The third technique will be the rear naked choke. This is our main flowchart of techniques to execute our strategy to finish the fight with a rear naked choke.

The note cards you created in a previous chapter will be the elements that make up your flowchart. You will place your *single leg takedown* note card on a table or wall first. Then to the right of that card you will place the *take the back* note card. The third card to the right will be the *rear naked choke* note card. Now you have three note cards in sequential order that make up your main strategy. Once you have the simple flowchart laid out, you can start to add contingency plans to the chart. For example, what happens if you cannot secure a single leg takedown? You will need to shift to a double leg takedown. On your flowchart you would place the double leg takedown note card directly below the single leg takedown card. Nothing else changes on the flowchart other than the opening technique.

What happens if you secure the takedown, but you cannot take their back? Now you have to place the *twisting arm control* note card in front of the *take the back* card. Hopefully you're starting to see the point of the flowchart. It allows us to externalize our strategy using note cards so that we can determine all the possible contingencies we will have to account for in a fight. In a dream world your original strategy is unchallenged, and you effortlessly submit your opponent. This is a quick victory, and it was possible back in the early days of jiu-jitsu. Now there are millions of people watching jiu-jitsu defense techniques in the UFC. It would be naive of us to think that our original strategy will work every time.

The more detailed our flowchart becomes the easier it will be to defeat our opponents. Again, most trained martial artists are only one to two steps ahead of an untrained person. If my flowchart extends to ten techniques from numerous variations, you are going to have a very long day trying to defeat me. I can tell you right now the average person will not be able to complete this step. Flowcharts and strategies are not for lazy people. This is the stage of memory development where champions shine and the mediocre fade away.

It will be up to you to decide how you want to construct your flowchart. I recommend laying your note cards out and taking a picture of them. This will allow you to create hundreds of flowcharts with the same note cards. You can also use colored markers on a dry-erase board to write out your flowchart. If you want to create a digital flowchart, that will work as well. You are only limited by your imagination. Hopefully you have activated your right brain enough in previous chapters to be able to create a flowchart that is unique to your own style. You are your own teacher.

Once you have created your flowchart you can use one of the memory techniques in previous chapters to memorize it. I like to place each technique from my flowchart in my house from left to right. If I add a contingency to the flowchart, I will place it below the object in my house. If I run out of objects from top to bottom, I will move on to a different part of my house. I never record over techniques that are already associated with objects in my house. I will find a new section of my house or use a different house altogether.

I use my vehicle for street fighting strategies. Every object on my Jeep has a technique associated with it in a sequential order according to my strategy. Because I'm more likely to have an altercation on the road, I have all my techniques fresh in my mind every time I go for a drive. Now that you have chosen to become your own shepherd, you will think of hundreds of new ways to create and memorize your strategies.

It has been my pleasure to share with you the memory techniques that I have used to learn jiu-jitsu. It is my hope that you will far surpass my own skills and reach levels that are currently unheard of. You have all the tools you need, and it will only be a matter of time before you discover what you're truly capable of. Until our paths cross again, good luck with your journey, and I'm glad I could play a small role in it.

In Summary:

1) Organize your note cards from left to right to create a flowchart for your basic strategy.

2) Add note cards under your basic strategy to account for contingencies.

3) Memorize your strategy using one of the memory techniques you learned in previous chapters.

Appendix: Sample Mind Map

Disclaimer:

This was my first mind map for jiu-jitsu. It covers the first thirty-six lessons I learned at Gracie University®. This mind map will serve as a good example of what your first mind map might look like. The techniques were memorized in the linear order they were taught in and not by body position. This map comes directly from my own training journal and has not been professionally edited. I did not want to change any words or punctuation for fear of losing the integrity of the original map.

Gracie University now offers a new Gracie Combatives 2.0 course. This course offers additional techniques and features that my notes do not cover. My notes only cover their original techniques from the first course.

If you want to actually learn the techniques in my mind map, you will need to sign up for the Gracie Combatives® course at GracieUniversity.com or visit a Certified Gracie Jiu-Jitsu Training Center. The instructions they provide offer details that you will not find in my notes. Certain aspects of their techniques that I could easily remember did not make it into my notes. My notes are unique to my own interpretation of their techniques. You may choose to use different words or even a different order to list the steps. The only way to properly memorize the techniques in my mind map is to learn them directly from the source.

White Belt Mind Map:

Lesson 1-A: Trap and Roll Escape (top of primary bedroom door)

Visual:

A dinner roll is stuck to a flytrap that is attached to a fire escape on top of the bedroom door. I reach up and grab the fire escape with my right hand that is in the shape of a bear trap.

Directions:

If the opponent has their right hand on your chest or throat, trap their right wrist with your right hand using a thumbless grip. Keep your left elbow tucked in as you trap the back of their right elbow with your left hand in a full grip. Now trap the opponent's right leg with your left leg and place your right leg inside of their left leg. Bridge your hips up and roll over your left shoulder. Land on your knees in the opponent's guard with your head pressed down on their abdomen. Finish by trapping the opponent's hips with your elbows.

Abbr. Directions:

Trap their right wrist and tricep. Trap their right leg and clear your right leg. Roll over your left shoulder and onto your knees. Press your head into their abdomen and trap their hips with your elbows.

Fill In the Word:

T t r w a t. T t r l a c y r l. R o y l s a o y k. P y h i t a a t t h w y e.

Linking Story:

The opponent's right hand is on my chest, so my right hand turns into a metal bear trap that clamps down on their right wrist. Now my left hand turns into a bear trap that I clamp onto the back of their right elbow. When the bear trap clamps down on the opponent's right elbow, honey sprays out of their arm and onto their right leg. My left leg then gets stuck to the honey on the opponent's right leg. As the opponent fights to get their leg unstuck from my leg, they accidentally press down on a switch that is attached to an airbag that is under my hips. The airbag goes off and my hips explode upward so I roll over a dinner roll that's on my left shoulder and end up on top of them. The honey on the opponent's right leg now gets stuck to the back of my elbows. My elbows then get stuck to the opponent's hips and they cannot get away.

Fill In the Story:

Bear traps, leg honey, airbag, dinner roll, and elbow honey.

Lesson 1-B: Punch Block Variation (left side of primary bedroom door)

Visual:

A cheerleader punches a concrete cinder block with her pom-poms on the left side of the bedroom door. Then a bear runs up and tackles her to the ground to get a hug.

Directions:

If the opponent is in top mount and they sit up to punch you, immediately sit up and bear hug them with both of your arms under their arms. Keep your head and chest pressed against their chest. Push off of your feet to pull the opponent down to the ground with you. Now grip the back of the opponent's shoulders and slide your body north using your feet and hands. Swim your left hand through the inside of opponent's right arm and wrap your left arm around their right arm. Grab the opponent's right tricep with your left hand and pin their arm down with your left side armpit. Then trap their right leg with your left leg and finish with the steps of the previous variation from here.

Abbreviated Directions:

Bear hug their body and pull them down. Slide north and wrap their right arm. Trap their right leg and clear your right leg. Roll over your left shoulder and onto your knees. Press your head into their abdomen and trap their hips with your elbows.

Word Fill:

B h t b a p t d. S n a w t r a. T t r l a c y r l. R o y l s a o y k. P y h i t a a t t h w y e.

Linking Story:

A grizzly bear is mounted on top of me and they are trying to slash me with their claws. I sit up and give them a bear hug and pull them down to the ground. I then grab the bears shoulders and slide north on a frozen water slide. I have a bear trap under my left side armpit so I clamp it down on their front right leg. When the trap clamps down it sprays honey all over the bears right leg. My left leg then gets stuck to the bear's right leg. As the bear fights to get their right leg unstuck from my leg, they accidentally press down on a switch that is attached to an airbag that is under my hips. The airbag goes off and my hips explode upwards, so I roll over a dinner roll on my left shoulder and land on top of the bear. The honey on the bear's legs now gets stuck to the back of my elbows and the bear cannot get away.

Fill In the Story:

Bear hug, water slide, bear trap, honey leg, airbag, dinner roll, and honey elbows.

Lesson 1-C: Headlock Variation (right side of primary bedroom door)

Visual:

A cheerleader has a padlock around her neck on the right side of the door. I try to unlock it with my left hand that is in the shape of a metal bear trap.

Directions:

If the opponent has you in a headlock with their right arm from top mount, trap their right arm with your left hand by grabbing the back of their right tricep or shoulder. Keep your head pressed against the ground to prevent them from getting their right arm free. Trap their right leg with your left leg and finish with the steps of the previous variation from here.

Abbreviated Directions:

Trap their right head locking arm and press your head onto the ground. Trap their right leg and clear your right leg. Roll over your left shoulder and onto your knees. Press your head into their abdomen and trap their hips with your elbows.

Fill In the Word:

T t r h l a a p y h o t g. T t r l a c y r l. R o y l s a o y k. P y h i t a a t t h w y e.

Linking Story:

The opponent's right arm is in the shape of a padlock and it's around my neck. My left hand turns into a bear trap that clamps down on the shackle of their right padlock arm. When the bear trap clamps down on the opponent's right padlock arm, honey sprays out of the lock and onto their right leg. My left leg then gets stuck to the honey on the opponent's right leg. As the opponent fights to get their right leg unstuck from my left leg, they accidentally press down on a switch that is attached to an airbag that is under my hips. The airbag goes off and my hips explode upward so I roll over a dinner roll on my left shoulder and land on top of the opponent. The honey on the opponent's right leg now gets stuck to the back of my elbows and the opponent cannot get away.

Fill In the Story:

Padlock, bear trap, honey leg, airbag, dinner roll, and honey elbows.

Lesson 1-D: Open Guard Pass (bottom of primary bedroom door)

Visual:

A British guard pushes the bottom of the door open and passes through the doorway. I immediately tackle him to the ground and hold him down with a turkey wishbone.

Directions: From the top of guard, push the opponent's right leg toward your left side and slide your left shin on top of their right thigh. Reach up and hug the back of their neck with your left arm. Now place your head on the left side of their head. Then pull your right leg across their left thigh and hook their left leg with your right leg. Finish by sliding your left shin across their right thigh and hook their right leg with your left leg to establish top mount.

Abbreviated Directions:

From the top of guard, push their right leg down and trap it with your left shin. Hug their neck with your left arm and place your head on the ground. Hook their left leg with your right leg. Finish by hooking their right leg with your left leg to establish top mount.

Fill In the Word:

F t t o g, p t r l d a t i w y l s. H t n w y l a a p y h o t g. H t l l w y r l. F b h t r l w y l l t e t m.

Linking Story: I'm holding down a British guard with my head and arms from the top guard position. I force his right leg over toward my left side and his right hip snaps into two pieces like a turkey wishbone. I immediately slide my left shin that is wearing a banana peel over his right thigh to pin it down. I now reach up and hook the back of his neck with my bailing hook left arm and it knocks off his big helmet. I then press my head that has a shovel on top of it into the ground on the left side of his head. My right arm extends out toward my right side and I dig my right shovel shaped hand into the ground. The guard now has a saddle on his abdomen. I pull my right leg all the way across his left leg and hook it into the right side stirrup. I then slide my left shin that is holding down the guard's right thigh across their leg and hook it into the left side stirrup. I'm now fully in the saddle with both stirrups hooking the guard's legs.

Fill In the Story:

British guard, wishbone, banana peel, bailing hook, shovel head, shovel hand, saddle, and stirrups.

Lesson 2-A: Americana Armlock (left side lamp shade)

Visual:

A mannequin arm with an American flag wrapped around it is handcuffed to the left side lamp shade. I break the handcuffs open with a bowling pin.

Directions:

From the top mount position, pin the opponent's left wrist down to the ground with your left hand and pin their left elbow down with your right hand. Now lower your left elbow down next to the left side of the opponent's head. Then slide your right hand palm up under the opponent's left tricep and grab the top of your left wrist. Hook the opponent's right leg with your left leg and extend your right knee out for base. Finish the armlock by dragging their left hand south along the ground.

Abbreviated Directions:

From the top mount position, pin their left wrist and elbow down. Place your left elbow on the ground. Slide your right hand palm up and grab your left wrist. Hook their right leg and brace with your right knee. Finish by dragging their left hand south.

Fill In the Word:

F t t m p, p t l w a e d. P y l e o t g. S y r h p u a g y l w. H t r l a b w y r k. F b d t l h s.

Linking Story:

The opponent is lying on their back and I'm sitting on a saddle that is cinched to their abdomen. The opponent's left forearm turns into a bowling pin. I grab the neck of the bowling pin which is the opponent's wrist and pin it to the ground with my left hand. I then use my right hand to press down on the base of the bowling pin which is the opponent's left elbow. My left elbow now turns into a knife that I slice down the left side of the opponent's face. Now I let go of the opponent's left elbow with my right hand and my right arm turns into a monkey's arm. I slide my right monkey hand palm up under the opponent's left tricep and hook the top of my left wrist with a thumbless grip. I then hook the opponent's right leg with my left stirrup and brace with my right knee that is wearing red brace. I finish by dragging the top of the opponent's bowling pin right hand south along the ground.

Fill In the Story:

Saddle, bowling pin, knife, monkey palm, stirrup, red knee brace, and bowling pin top.

Lesson 2-B: Neck Hug Variation (left side lamp base)

Visual:

A cheerleader with a bear cub around her neck is standing with her arms in a V formation at the base of the left side lamp. Her left arm is in the shape of a bowling pin.

Directions:

If the opponent is too combative for the standard variation, hug the back of their neck with your left arm and grab their left wrist with your right hand. Slide the opponent's left wrist over to your left hand and grab their left wrist with your left hand. Now slide your right hand palm up under their left tricep and grab your left wrist. Hook the opponent's right leg with your left leg and extend your right knee out for base. Unhook your left arm from behind the opponent's neck and place your left elbow next to the left side of their head. Finish the armlock by dragging their left hand south along the ground.

Abbreviated Directions:

From the top mount position, hug their neck with your left arm. Slide their left wrist over to your left hand and grab it. Slide your right hand palm up and grab your left wrist. Hook their right leg and brace with your right knee. Unhook your left arm and place it next to their head. Finish by dragging their left hand south.

Fill In the Word:

F t t m p, h t n w y l a. S t l w o t y l h a g i. S y r h p u a g y l w. H t r l a b w y r k. U y l a a p i n t t h. F b d t l h s.

Linking Story:

The opponent is lying on their back and I'm sitting on a saddle that is cinched to their abdomen. The opponent's head turns into a bear's head so I hug the back of their neck with my left arm. The opponent's left arm then turns into a bowling pin. I grab the neck of the bowling pin which is the opponent's left wrist and pin it to the ground with my right hand. I then slide the neck of the bowling pin over to my left hand that is behind the bear's neck and grab it with my left hand. My right arm now turns into a monkey's arm and I slide my right monkey hand palm up under the opponents left tricep. Now I hook the top of my left wrist with my right hand in a thumbless grip. I then hook the opponent's right leg with my left stirrup and extend my right knee that is wearing a red brace out for base. Then I slide my left arm out from behind the bear's neck that is covered in fish oil and place my left elbow next to the left side of their head. I finish by dragging the top of the bowling pin backwards along the ground until the opponent yells stop.

Fill In the Story:

Saddle, bear head, bowling pin, monkey palm, stirrup, red knee brace, fish oil, and bowling pin top.

Lesson 3: Positional Control - Top Mount (left side night stand)

Visual:

A person is using a compass while they ride a horse with reins on top of the nightstand. A bald eagle flies down and scares the horse causing it to rear up and flip over backwards.

Directions:

From the top mount position, establish leg hooks with your hips low and pressed heavily into the opponent. Brace both of your arms out wide. If the opponent tries to roll toward your right side, brace out with your right arm at a forty-five-degree angle and hug their neck with your left arm. Hook their right leg with your left leg and brace out with your right knee. If the opponent tries to break down your right arm, rotate your right forearm in a clockwise circle and re-establish the arm brace. If the opponent bench presses you upwards, go to your knees, and place all of your weight onto their hands. Raise your left shoulder up to release the weight from their right hand. Now swim your left arm inside of their right arm and push their arm to the outside. Place your hand back down on the ground for base but keep it close to the opponent's body so you have the height needed to clear your other arm. Repeat the lift and swim procedure for your other arm. Finish by lowering your upper body down and hugging their neck with one of your arms. This will prevent the opponent from bench pressing you up again.

Abbreviated Directions:

From the top mount position, establish leg hooks and brace with your arms. If they roll toward your right side, brace with your right arm and hug their neck with your left arm. Hook their right leg and brace with your right knee. Circle your right arm if needed. If they push you up, raise your shoulders and swim your arms inside. Finish by lowering your body and hugging their neck.

Fill In the Word:

F t t m p, e l h a b w y a. I t r t y r s, b w y r a a h t n w y l a. H t r l a b w y r k. C y r a i n. I t p y u, r y s a s y a i. F b l y b a h t n.

Linking Story:

My body is transformed into a bald eagle and I land on a saddle that is cinched to the stomach of a horse who is lying on its back on the ground. My wings spread out to prevent the horse from rolling over and my talons hook the horse's hind legs. When the horse tries to roll toward my right side, my right wing spreads out for base, and my left wing wraps behind the horse's neck. My left talon hooks the horse's right hind leg while my right talon stretches out for base. If the horse tries to move my right bracing wing, I will circle the wing in a clockwise direction to maintain the brace. If the horse bench presses me upward, I will place all of my weight onto their front hooves and lift one shoulder up at a time while I swim my water drenched wing inside of their front leg to re-establish a brace. After I have escaped both of the hooves, I will take one of my bracing wings and wrap it behind the horse's neck to prevent them from bench pressing me up again.

Fill In the Story:

Bald eagle, saddle, wings, talons, wing, horse neck, clock, bench, hooves, water, and horse neck.

Lesson 4-A: Take the Back - Top Mount (top of headboard)

Visual:

A baby is sitting on top of a horse on top of the headboard with a banana shaped sucker stuck to their back. A gorilla takes the piece of candy and eats it.

Directions:

You will need to modify your mount if the opponent is able to turn over to their left side while you are in top mount. Once the opponent is in motion to get to their left side, quickly slide your right knee north. Now slide your right heel inward and rest it against the opponent's abdomen. Your left knee should be resting against the back of the opponent's head with your lower left leg running down along their back. Place both hands on the ground slightly north of the opponent's shoulders and brace them firmly. As the opponent gets onto their knees, hook their legs with your legs but do not cross your feet. Your weight should now be entirely on your toes and hands as you rock your body backward. Stay as low on the opponent's back as possible to avoid getting shook off. If you touch the opponent's back as you slide south it may create friction that can slow the move down. Place your left arm over the opponent's left shoulder and your right arm under their right armpit. Place your head next to the right side of the opponent's head. Grip your palms together to lock in the hold. Now you will be able to stick to the opponent regardless of the direction they roll.

Abbreviated Directions:

From the top mount position, establish a modified mount and brace with your arms when the opponent turns onto their left side. When they roll onto their knees, establish leg hooks and brace with your arms. Push off your hands and rock backwards on your toes. Finish by establishing an over under grip and roll to one side.

Fill In the Word:

F t t m p, e a m m a b w y a w t o t o t l s. W t r o t k, e l h a b w y a. P o y h a r b o y t. F b e a o u g a r t o s.

Linking Story:

A silverback gorilla is mounted on a super model. The model turns onto her side to get up, so the gorilla presses his heel into her abdomen which crushes a banana that was lying in front of her abdomen. Then the gorilla slams his knee into the back of her head and shoulders which explodes another banana that was lying next to her head. His gorilla hands turn into shovels that dig into the ground for base. Now the model rolls onto her knees so the gorilla's legs turn into large fishhooks that hook her legs. The gorilla then balances on his shovel hands and toes. Now his feet turn into rocking chairs that he rocks back on before securing an over under grip like a baby monkey holding onto his mom's back.

Fill In the Story:

Gorilla, model, abdomen banana, head banana, shovels, fishhooks, rocking chairs, and baby monkey.

Lesson 4-B: Remount Technique (bottom of headboard)

Visual:

A person wearing black framed glasses slides off a horse at the bottom of the headboard because their saddle is covered in fish oil. The rider remounts the horse by swinging their tether ball leg over the saddle, but they immediately slip off again.

Directions:

If the opponent starts to slip away and turn towards their right side from the back mount position, unhook your bottom left leg and swing your right leg over their abdomen. Now pull your bottom left hand out from under their left armpit. Then pivot on your bottom left shoulder as you roll on top of the opponent. Brace with your arms to secure the top mount position. Your bottom left leg should straighten as you roll over, forcing it to end up on the outside of the opponent's right leg.

Abbreviated Directions:

From the back mount position, unhook your left leg and swing your right leg over their abdomen. Pull your left hand out and pivot on your left shoulder. Straighten your left leg as you roll on top of the opponent. Brace with your arms to secure top mount.

Fill In the Word:

F t b m p, u y l l a s y r l o t a. P y l h o a p o y l s. S y l l a y r o t o t o. B w y a t s t m.

Linking Story:

The opponent's body is covered in fish oil so they are able to slip away and roll toward me. I immediately release my bottom left fishhook leg from their left leg that is closest to the ground. My top right leg turns into a tether ball that swings over the opponent's abdomen and digs into the ground. Now I slip my bottom left hand that is wrapped in a banana peel out from underneath their left armpit. Then I balance on my left shoulder that is resting on a gymnastics balance beam. I finish by straightening my left leg that is made from an arrow and roll on top of the opponent who is wearing a saddle. I finish by digging my shovel hands into the ground to secure the top mount position.

Fill In the Story:

Fish oil, fishhook, tether ball, banana peel, balance beam, arrow, saddle, and shovels.

Lesson 5-A: Rear Naked Choke (top of footboard)

Visual: A naked person is lying face down on top of the footboard and they are getting choked by a snake that slithered out from under the comforter.

Directions: From behind the opponent, wrap your right arm around their neck and keep your right elbow pressed tightly under their chin. Now wrap your right hand around the back of your left tricep. Then take your left hand and slide it behind the opponent's head using either side of your hand. Look toward your left elbow and press the right side of your head into your left hand that is behind the opponent's skull. Once the choke is in place squeeze your shoulders backward using your back muscles and not your arms. Your chest should press into the opponent as you squeeze backwards.

Abbreviated Directions:

From behind the opponent, wrap your right arm around their neck. Hook your left tricep with your right hand. Slide your left hand behind their head and press your face into it. Finish by squeezing your shoulders backward.

Fill In the Word:

F b t o, w y r a a t n. H y l t w y r h. S y l h b t h a p y f i i. F b s y s b.

Linking Story:

I'm on the back of an opponent and my right arm turns into a Boa Constrictor snake that slithers under the opponent's neck and bites the back of my left tricep. My left hand is covered in blood from the bite so it easily slides behind the opponent's head. I press the right side of my face into my left hand that is holding a whip cream pie. I have the back of a Silverback gorilla, so I use it to arch backward as I smash a banana on my chest and finish the choke.

Fill In the Story:

Snake, blood, pie, Silver Back gorilla, and banana.

Lesson 5-B: Strong Side Variation (right side of footboard)

Visual:

A muscular cheerleader is flexing her big bicep in a sideways pose on the right side of the footboard when a snake bites her left tricep.

Directions:

From the strong right side position, use your top left hand that is under the opponent's left armpit to grab their left wrist. Wrap your bottom right arm around their neck as tight as possible. If the opponent's chin is not in line with your right elbow, you can let go of their left wrist, and use your left fist to press or punch their face into position. Once your right arm is securely around the opponent's neck, pull your left arm out from under their left armpit. Hook your right hand around your left tricep and slide your left hand behind their head. Press the right side of your face into your left hand. Finish by squeezing your shoulders backward as you push your chest forward.

Abbreviated Directions:

From the strong right side position, grab their left wrist with your left hand. Wrap your right arm around their neck. Pull your left arm out and hook your left tricep with your right hand. Slide your left hand behind their head and press your face into it. Finish by squeezing your shoulders backward.

Fill In the Word:

F t s r s p, g t l w w y l h. W y r a a t n. P y l a o a h y l t w y r h. S y l h b t h a p y f i i. F b s y s b.

Linking Story:

My left hand turns into a bear trap that clamps down on the opponent's left wrist. My right arm turns into a Boa Constrictor snake that wraps around the opponent's neck. My left bear trap hand releases the opponent's left wrist and slips out from under their oily armpit. My right snake arm that is around the opponent's neck bites the back of my left tricep. The blood from the bite makes it easy to slide my left hand behind the opponent's head. I press the right side of my face into a whip cream pie that is in my left hand. I have the back of a Silverback gorilla, so I use it to squeeze my shoulders backward as I smash a banana on my chest and finish the choke.

Fill In the story:

Bear trap, snake, oil, snake bite, blood, pie, Silverback gorilla, and banana.

Lesson 5-C: Weak Side Variation (left side of footboard)

Visual:

A skinny cheerleader is flexing her small bicep in a sideways pose on the left side of the footboard when a snake bites her right tricep.

Directions:

From the weak left side position, wrap the opponent's neck with your top right arm and grab their bottom left shoulder. Pull up on their bottom left shoulder at the same time you pull on their top right leg with your top right leg hook. This will allow you to roll the opponent over enough to pull out your trapped left arm out from under their left armpit. Now use your bottom left arm to switch places with your top right arm under the opponent's neck. Then hook your left hand around your right tricep. Slide your right hand behind their head and press the left side of your face against it. Finish by squeezing your shoulders backward as you push your chest forward.

Abbreviated Directions:

From the weak left side position, wrap their neck and grab their left shoulder. Pull up on their left shoulder and right leg. Slide your left arm out and place it under their neck. Hook your left hand around your right tricep. Slide your right hand behind their head and press your face into it. Finish by squeezing your shoulders backward.

Fill In the Word:

F t w l s p, w t n a g t l s. P u o t l s a r l. S y l a o a p i u t n. H y l h a y r t. S y r h b t h a p y f i i. F b s y s b.

Linking Story:

My top right arm turns into a snake that slithers under the opponent's neck and bites their bottom left shoulder. My top right foot is wearing a boot with a razor-sharp spur that digs into the opponent's top right leg. Now I pull the opponent over enough to slip my bottom left arm out from under the opponent's oily left armpit. Now my bottom left arm turns into a snake and slithers under my top right snake arm before it bites the back of my right arm's tricep. Now my top right snake arm turns into a banana peel and slides behind the opponent's head. Then I press the left side of my face against my right banana peel hand that is holding a whip cream pie. I have the back of a Silverback gorilla, so I use it to squeeze my shoulders backward as I smash a banana on my chest and finish the choke.

Fill In the Story:

Snake, snake bite, spur, oil, snake, snake bite, banana peel, pie, Silverback gorilla, and banana.

Lesson 6: Leg Hook Takedown (right side lamp)

Visual:

A person with knives mounted on their arms knocks the lamp down with their hook leg.

Directions:

If the opponent throws a punch, kick, or is taking a step toward you with their left leg forward, shoot in with your left leg forward and your hands up by your face. Press the left side of your face against their chest as you wrap your left arm behind their back. Reach across the front of their waist with your right arm and hook your left wrist with your right hand to establish the clinch. Step to the outside of their right foot with your left foot and place your right foot in front of both their feet. Now Take one small step toward the opponent with your right foot and squeeze their body tightly. Hook their right calf with your left calf and pull their right leg up between your legs. Then lean forward to take them down. On the way down to the ground, bring your left leg forward to help slow the fall. Release your hand grip and brace with your arms as you land on top of the opponent in half guard. Finish by hooking their left leg with your right leg to establish top mount.

Abbreviated Directions:

Step forward with your left leg and block your face. Press your face against their chest as you wrap your arms around their waist. Adjust your feet and hook their right calf with your left calf. Lean forward to take them down. Slow the fall with your left leg and brace with your arms. Finish by hooking their left leg to establish top mount.

Fill In the Word:

S f w y l l a b y f. P y f a t c a y w y a a t w. A y f a h t r c w y l c. L f t t t d. S t f w y l l a b w y a. F b h t l l t e t m.

Linking Story:

The opponent throws a punch at me, so I shoot in with knife blades mounted to my forearms. The blades go all the way through the opponent's chest, so I slide my arms out of the mounts and wrap them around their waist like an Anaconda snake. I shuffle my feet across playing cards on the ground to get my feet into position. My left calf has a razaor-sharp spur attached to it that I dig into the right calf of the opponent and pull their right leg between my legs. Then I lean forward to take the opponent down to the ground. My left foot is wearing a turtle shell shoe that I extend forward to slow the fall down. I let go of the opponent's waist and brace the fall with my eagle wing arms. The knife blades coming out the back of the opponent stick into the ground and the opponent is trapped underneath me in half mount. I notice that a saddle is cinched to the opponent's abdomen, so I hook their left leg as I put my right foot into the stirrup to establish top mount.

Fill In the Story:

Knives, snake, cards, spur, turtle shell, wings, knives, saddle, and stirrup.

Lesson 7: Clinch with Aggressive Opponent (right side night stand)

Visual: A person clinches their teeth down on a bear's honey drenched chest as the bear tries to attack them on the right side nightstand.

Directions: Stay two arm lengths away from the opponent, If the opponent throws a punch, kick, or is taking a step toward you with their left leg forward, shoot in with your left leg forward and your hands up by your face. Press the left side of your face against their chest as you wrap your left arm behind their back. Reach across the front of their waist with your right arm and hook your left wrist with your right hand to establish the clinch. Step to the outside of their right foot with your left foot and place your right foot in front of both their feet to establish a strong base. Finish with a takedown.

Abbreviated directions:

Stay two arm lengths away from the opponent. When they step forward with their left leg, block your face and shoot in with your left leg forward. Press your face against their chest and wrap your arms around their waist. Establish a base with your feet and finish with a takedown.

Fill In the Word:

S t a l a f t o. W t s f w t l l, b y f a s i w y l l f. P y f a t c a w y a a
t w. E a b w y f a f w a t.

Linking Story: A raging bear with honey on his chest runs toward me on his hind legs. I'm waving two measuring sticks that are taped together to keep him back. Now I cover my face with two large oversized boxing gloves and shoot into his chest. My face gets stuck to his chest because of the honey. Then my arms turn into snakes that quickly wrap around his waist. I shuffle my feet across playing cards to establish base. I finish by taking the bear down on soft grass.

Fill In the Story:

Bear, measuring stick, boxing gloves, honey, snakes, cards, and grass.

Lesson 8: Punch Block Series (top of window)

Visual:

A boxing glove is sitting on top of a concrete cinderblock that is sitting on top of a baseball bat on top of the window.

Lesson 8-A: Stage 1 (left side of window)

Visual: A stagecoach with one horse hitched to it is being driven by a spider monkey on the left side of the window.

Directions:

From the bottom of guard, hook your legs high around the opponent's back and cross your feet to establish a closed guard. Pull the opponent's head down next to the right side of your face with your right hand. Now wrap your left arm around their right arm to trap it under your left side armpit. Keep your head bent forward off of the ground and press it into the right side of the opponent's head. Press your left forearm into your left thigh to prevent them from pulling their arm away and punching you. If the opponent gets their right arm free, quickly swim your left arm back into position and press your left forearm even tighter against your left thigh to prevent them from pulling it out again. Keep both of your knees pulled in close to your elbows to prevent the opponent from punching you. If the opponent pulls down your right hand from the back of their head, quickly switch hands to keep their head held down. Then trap their left arm with your right arm. Conserve your energy in this position and allow the opponent to become tired.

Abbreviated Directions:

From the bottom guard position, cross your feet behind their back. Pull their head down with your right hand and wrap your left arm around their right arm. Press the right side of your head against the right side of their head. Finish by pressing your elbows against your knees.

Fill In the Word:

F t b g p, c y f b t b. P t h d w y r h a w y l a a t r a. P t r s o y h a
t r s o t h. F b p y e a y k.

Linking Story:

My body turns into a baby spider monkey, and I wrap my legs around the opponent's body and cross my feet behind their back. I hold the back of the opponent's head down with my right hand that is covered in hair gel. I use my left arm to pin their right arm down with a bear trap that is under my left armpit. The bear trap punctures their skin and sprays honey onto the right side of my head and the back of my elbows. This causes my head to get stuck to the opponent's head and my elbows to get stuck to my knees.

Fill In the Story:

Monkey, hair gel, bear trap, and honey.

Lesson 8-B: Stage 2 (right side of window)

Visual:

A stagecoach with two horses hitched to it is being driven by a spider monkey who has honey stuck to his hands on the right side of the window.

Directions:

If the opponent pulls their right arm out, fill the space by pressing your left knee against the inside of their right arm and hold onto the back of their right tricep with your left hand. Do the same thing with the opponent's other arm if they are trying to punch you with it. Let the opponent struggle and punch their self out. When they start to weaken and get heavy, lower their body down with your legs in a controlled way to resume stage one. The opponent must be leaning toward you for this technique to work.

Abbreviated Directions:

If they pull their right arm out, hook their right tricep with your left hand. Press your left knee against their right bicep. Repeat the process on their left arm if needed. Finish by lowering them back down into stage one.

Fill In the Word:

I t p t r a o, h t r t w y l h. P y l k a t r b. R t p o t l a i n. F b l t b d i s o.

Linking Story:

The opponent is able to pull their right arm out from under my left bear trap armpit. Their right tricep is covered in honey so I my left hand gets stuck to their right tricep. My left knee has a metal spike attached to it, so I drive it through the opponent's right bicep. Now the opponent treies to punch me with their left arm so I repeat the process on the other side. Once they get tired from wearing the Sleeper Hold® travel pillow, I lower them back down into stage one.

Fill In the Story:

Bear trap, honey, metal spike, and travel pillow.

Lesson 8-C: Stage 3 (bottom of window)

Visual:

A stagecoach with three horses hitched to it is being driven by a spider monkey with spike knee pads at the bottom of the window.

Directions:

If the opponent breaks free from the stage two position, immediately push them back with your arms to create enough space to get your knees on their chest. Place both of your knees close together on the opponent's chest with your feet outside of their hips for control. Keep your hips elevated to create enough distance to keep them from punching you. Once the opponent puts enough weight onto your knees, protect your face and lower them back down into stage one.

Abbreviated Directions:

From the stage two position, push the opponent back with your arms and place your knees on their chest. Place your feet on their hips and elevate your hips. Finish by blocking your face and lowering their body down.

Fill In the Word:

F t s t p, p t o b w y a a p y k o t c. P y f o t h a e y h. F b b y f a l t b d.

Linking Story:

The opponent breaks free from my stage two straitjacket hold. I push the opponent back with my arms that are in the shape of bulldozers and stick my spiked knee pads into their chest. Then my feet hold down two pistols that are in holsters on their hips. I then widen my knees and lower their body back down into stage one as I block my face with oversized boxing gloves.

Fill In the Story:

Straitjacket, bulldozers, spike knee pads, pistols, and boxing gloves.

Lesson 8-D: Stage 4 (window blinds)

Visual:

A stagecoach with four horses hitched to it is being driven by a spider monkey and frog at the center of the blinds.

Directions:

If at any point the opponent starts to stand up from one of the previous stages, push them back with your arms and place your feet on their waist. Place your heels in the center of their waist and point your toes outward. Keep your knees slightly bent and only hold the opponent back for one or two punches. Finish by blocking your face as you lower the opponent back down into stage one.

Abbreviated Directions:

If the opponent starts to stand up, push them back with your arms and place your feet on their waist. Finish by blocking your face and lowering them back down into stage one.

Fill In the Word:

I t o s t s u, p t b w y a a p y f o t w. F b b y f a l t b d i s o.

Linking Story:

The opponent starts to stand up, so I push them away with my long spider monkey arms. After I have pushed the opponent away, my legs turn into frog legs, and I stick my webbed frog feet on their waist. I now protect my face with large, oversized boxing gloves as I lower the opponent back down into stage one.

Fill In the Story:

Spider monkey arms, frog legs, webbed feet, and boxing gloves.

Lesson 9-A: Straight Armlock – Top Mount (top of television)

Visual:

A person with an arrow stuck into their arm dies while riding a horse with their arm handcuffed to a saddle on top of the television.

Directions:

If the opponent's arms are extended upwards when you are in the top mount position, place your left arm on the north side of their right arm and your right arm on the south side. Point your fingers toward the left side of their chest. Now point your right foot out toward the right side and place it close to the opponent's left armpit. Then pivot on your hands as you spin your left leg around to the left side of the opponent's head and sit down. Trap their right wrist with both of your hands. Keep your legs bent and firm as you lean back and pull the opponent's right arm toward your right shoulder with their thumb facing up. Finish the armlock by pressing down on their right wrist as you elevate your hips against their right elbow.

Abbreviated Directions:

From the top mount position, place your hands on their chest. Step forward with your right foot. Pivot on your hands as you swing your left leg around their head and sit down. Pull their right wrist toward your right shoulder. Finish by elevating your hips.

Fill In the Word:

F t t m p, p y h o t c. S f w y r f. P o y h a y s y l l a t h a s d. P t r w t y r s. F b e y h.

Linking Story:

I'm sitting on a saddle that is on top of the opponent. The opponent dies so I place my hands on their chest with my fingers pointing away from their right arm and I perform CPR chest compressions. The opponent comes back to life, so my right foot that is wearing a cowboy boot steps forward. My hands have knives mounted to them that dig into the opponent's chest. Then my left leg turns into a helicopter blade that I swing around to the left side of their head. Now I grab the opponent's right wrist with both of my bear trap hands and extend their arm toward my right shoulder that is on fire. I finish by lifting my groin to crack a walnut that is stuck to the back of their right elbow.

Fill In the Story:

Saddle, CPR, boot, knives, helicopter blade, bear traps, fire, and walnut.

Lesson 9-B: Modified Mount Variation (bottom of television)

Visual:

A supermodel and a silver back gorilla are riding a horse with their arms in a V formation at the bottom of the television.

Directions:

With the opponent on their left side in your modified mount, hook the opponent's top right arm with your southern right arm. Walk your right foot that is in front of the opponent's abdomen north until it's under the opponent's bottom left side armpit. Now press down on the right side of the opponent's head with your left hand. Lean south and spin your left leg around to the front side of their face and sit down. Trap their right wrist with both of your hands. Keep your legs bent and firm as you lean back and pull the opponent's right arm toward your right shoulder with their thumb facing up. Finish the armlock by pressing down on their right wrist as you elevate your hips against their right elbow.

Abbreviated Directions:

From the modified mount position, hook their right arm with your right arm. Walk your right foot north. Press your left hand on their head as you spin your left leg around their head and sit down. Pull their right wrist back toward your right shoulder. Finish by elevating your hips.

Fill In the Word:

F t m m p, h t r a w y r a. W y r f n. P y l h o t h a y s y l l a t h a s d. P t r w b t y r s. F b e y h.

Linking Story:

A Silverback gorilla has a super model in a left side modified mount position. The gorilla's southern right arm turns into a fiery bailing hook that he uses to hook the model's top right arm. The gorilla's right foot that is in front of model's abdomen has a dog leash attached to it. His right foot starts to walk north towards the model's armpit, and it gets stuck to her armpit with deodorant that is made from glue. The gorilla uses his left hand to smash a whipped cream pie into the right side of her face and balances his body weight on the pie. Now he swings his northern left leg around the model's head like a helicopter blade and places it next to his other foot. The gorilla now uses both of his bear trap hands to grab the model's wrist and then he extends her arm. The model holds her thumb up and asks to hitch a ride to the gorilla's southern shoulder. Once the model arrives at the gorilla's southern shoulder, she still wants to fight so he lifts his groin and cracks a walnut that is stuck to the back of her elbow.

Fill In the Story:

Gorilla, bailing hook, dog leash, glue, pie, helicopter blade, bear traps, hitchhiker, and walnut.

Lesson 10-A: Triangle Choke (top of left side dresser)

Visual:

A large metal triangle is hanging from a noose on top of the dresser. A British guard is hanging from the triangle with a sack of potatoes around his neck.

Directions:

If you are on your back with the opponent in your guard, swing your right leg over their left shoulder and cross your legs behind their back. Grab the opponent's right wrist that is between your legs with both hands and pull it across your body. If the opponent does not let you pull their arm all the way across you can still finish the choke with their arm bent. You can also extend your hips upward to pull their right arm across then lower your hips back down to hold their arm in place. Now remove your left hand from the opponent's right wrist and place it behind their head. Pull down on the opponent's head with your left hand and hold their right wrist next to your right thigh with your right hand. Then uncross your feet from behind the opponent's back. Place your left foot onto their right hip and push against it as you walk north on your shoulders. You can also use your right thigh that is over the opponent's left shoulder to help push with. Walk your body north until your hips are directly under the opponent's neck. Now fold your right lower leg across the back of the opponent's neck and grab your right lower shin with your left hand. Then hook your left leg over your right ankle to lock in the hold. Finish by using both of your hands to press down on the back of their head as you elevate your hips and squeeze your knees together.

Abbreviated Directions:

From the bottom of guard, swing your right leg over their left shoulder and cross your legs. Pull their right wrist across your body and pull down on their head. Uncross your legs and push off your left foot to slide north. Place your right leg behind their neck and hook your left leg over it. Finish by pulling their head down as you elevate your hips and squeeze your knees together.

Fill In the Word:

F t b o g, s y r l o t l s a c y l. P t r w a y b a p d o t h. U y l a p o y l f t s n. P y r l b t n a h y l l o i. F b p t h d a y e y h a s y k t.

Linking Story:

A British guard is in my guard. My right leg turns into a long thin sack of potatoes. I swing my sack of potatoes over the British guard's left shoulder and cross my crucifix shaped legs behind their back. I then pull the British guard's right arm that is trapped inside of my legs across my body like I'm fastening a seat belt. I keep my right hand on the seat fastener which is the guard's right wrist and grab the back of the British guard's helmet with my left hand and hold it down. I uncross my feet and dig my left foot with a spike on the bottom of it into their right hip. I walk north on my shoulder blades across snow covered ground until my hips are directly under the British guard's neck. Now I sling my right leg that is made from a sack of potatoes behind the guard's neck and grab the bottom of it with my left hand. I then hook my left leg that is made from a bailing hook over the sack of potatoes to lock in the hold. I let go of the seat fastener with my right hand and place both of my hands on the back of the British guard's helmet. I press down on his helmet as I elevate my hips, and squeeze my knees together, until mashed potatoes come out his nose.

Fill In the Story:

Guard, potatoes, crucifix, seat belt, helmet, spike, snow, potatoes, bailing hook, helmet, and mashed potatoes.

Lesson 10-B: Punch Block Variation (left side of left side dresser)

Visual:

Mike Tyson throws a punch at a cheerleader, and she blocks it with her knee that has a knife attached to it.

Directions:

From the stage one point five position, slide your right hand from the back of the opponent's left tricep down along their arm and grab their left wrist. Push their left arm backward by pressing your right shin against their left arm at the same time you push their left wrist back. This will create a small gap for you to pull your right leg through. Your left leg should bite into the back of the opponent to help control them while you pull your right leg through. Once your right leg is through, swing it over their left shoulder to set up the standard triangle choke. If you are unable to pull your right leg through, straighten your right leg out and swing it all the way around until it hits your own right arm and hooks around the back of the opponent's neck. You will need to release your grip on the opponent's left wrist at the same time your right leg hits your right arm. If the opponent pulls their left wrist free, immediately swing your right leg over their left shoulder and cross your feet. Finish with the steps in the standard variation from here.

Abbreviated Directions:

From the stage one point five position, slide your right hand down and grab their left wrist. Push their left arm back and pull your right leg out. You can also swing your right leg around your right arm. Now swing your right leg over their left shoulder and cross your legs. Finish with the standard variation.

Fill In the Word:

F t s o p f p, s y r h d a g t l w. P t l a b a p y r l o. Y c a s y r l a y r a. N s y r l o t l s a c y l. F w t s v.

Linking Story:

I have Mike Tyson in stage one point five of the punch block series. I slide my right hand down Mike's left arm using the blood from the knife puncture in his left bicep. Then I grab his left wrist with my right bear trap hand. I push his left arm backward like a bulldozer until it's no longer stuck to the knife and. Now I pull my right leg through the gap and place it over his left shoulder like a sack of potatoes. If the gap is not big enough to get my right leg through, I will swing my right leg around like it's an iron chain that smashes across my right wrist and lays over his left shoulder. I finish by crossing my crucifix shaped legs behind his back and complete the rest of the standard variation steps from here.

Fill In the Story:

Tyson, blood, bear trap, bulldozer, potatoes, chain, and crucifix.

Lesson 10-C: Giant Killer Variation (right side of left side dresser)

Visual:

A cheerleader kills a giant basketball player with a basketball she slung out of a slingshot on the right side of the dresser.

Directions:

If the opponent is pressing down on you from guard, place your legs high up on their back before squeezing with your thighs and extending your legs south. Push against the right side of their head with both hands as you uncross your leg hooks and place your left foot on the ground. Shrimp your hips toward your left side by pivoting on your right shoulder and pressing against your left foot that is on the ground. You should now be lying on your right side. Now that you have space between you and the opponent place both of your feet onto their waist and return to your back. Grab the opponent's right wrist with both of your hands and hold it close to your chest. Use your feet to keep the opponent away from you. Retract your right leg while your left leg continues to hold the opponent back. In one movement, pull the opponent's wrist north as you swing your right leg over their left shoulder. Then place your left foot that is on the opponent's waist behind their back and cross your feet. Finish with the standard variation from here.

Abbreviated Directions:

From the bottom of guard, push the opponent south with your legs. Push against the right side of their head and place your left foot on the ground. Shrimp onto your right side and place your feet on their waist. Return to your back and pull their right wrist north as you swing your right leg over their left shoulder. Cross your legs and finish with the standard variation.

Fill In the Word:

Ftbog, ptoswyl. Patrsothapylfotg. Soyrsapyf otw. Rtybaptrwnaysyrlotls. Cylafwtsv.

Linking Story:

I have Shaquille O'Neal in my guard and he is pressing all of his weight down on me. I squeeze his upper back with my legs and push him down like an accordion. His head turns into a basketball that I push towards my right side. My back is resting on a giant shrimp that crawls toward my left side. Now that I'm lying on my right side, I place my feet with metal spikes on them into his waist. The shrimp then crawls back toward my right side and returns me to my back. My hands turn into bear traps that clamp down on his left wrist. I pull his wrist close to my chest and keep both of my arrow legs straight to keep his hips away from me. I then cock my right leg back like a rooster as my left arrow leg keeps him back. Now I pull his left arm north at the same time I swing my right rooster leg over his left shoulder. I then cross my crucifix shaped legs behind his back and finish with the standard variation from here.

Fill In the Story:

Shaq, accordion, basketball, shrimp, spikes, shrimp, bear traps, arrow, rooster leg, and crucifixes.

Lesson 11-A: Elevator Hook Sweep (top of left side bathroom door)

Visual:

A trapeze artist with a hook arm is sweeping out the inside of an elevator at the top of the door.

Directions:

If the opponent is in your closed guard and they have their left leg stretched out to the side with all of their weight on top of you. Place your right hand on the back of the opponent's head as your left arm pins down their right arm. Uncross your legs and pivot off of the opponent's left hip with your right leg. Then swing your hips out toward your right side. Circle your right lower leg around the opponent's left leg and hook their inner left thigh. Let go of the opponent's head with your right arm and slide it inside of their left arm. Now wrap your right arm around their back and reach toward the sky as you apply pressure on the opponent's left inner thigh with your right foot. This will start the process of rolling the opponent over toward your left side. Once the opponent starts to lift off of the ground, chop their right knee out from underneath them with your left leg. As you chop the opponent's right knee out, put all of your weight onto your left shoulder and use your right leg to roll them all the way over into a top mount position.

Abbreviated Directions:

From stage one of guard, pivot off their left hip and swing your hips out toward your right side. Circle your right leg around and hook the inside of their left thigh. Slide your right arm inside their left arm and reach upward with your right arm and leg. Chop their right leg out and pivot on your left shoulder as you roll over into top mount.

Fill In the Word:

F s o o g, p o t l h a s y h o t y r s. C y r l a a h t i o t l t. S y r a i t l a a r u w y r a a l. C t r l o a p o y l s a y r o i t m.

Linking Story:

A trapeze artist in tights is in my guard with her left leg stretched out to the side and the rest of her body weight on top of me. I hold her head down with my chalk covered right hand and my left arm has a bear trap under my armpit that is clamped down onto her right arm. My right leg turns into a swing that hangs from her left leg. I then swing my hips toward my right side. Once my hips have swung out to the right side, my right foot turns into a bailing hook, and I hook the inside of her left thigh with it. Now I slide my chalk covered right hand inside her left arm and around her back. I start to lift up on my right hook foot and reach toward the sky with my chalk covered right hand. Once the trapeze artist starts to lift off the ground, my left leg turns into a butcher's knife that chops her right knee out from underneath her. My left shoulder pivots on a balance beam as I roll her all the way over and sit on a saddle that is cinched to her abdomen.

Fill In the Story:

Trapeze artist, chalk, bear trap, swing, bailing hook, chalk, knife, balance beam, and saddle.

Lesson 11-B: Headlock Variation (bottom of left side bathroom door)

Visual:

A trapeze artist with her arms in a V formation has her head padlocked to the bottom of the door.

Directions:

If the opponent's trapped right arm gets free and they put you in a headlock with it, place your left hand on their right shoulder while your right hand continues to hold their head down. Uncross your legs and pivot off of the opponent's left hip as you swing your hips out toward your right side. Your right lower leg then circles around the opponent's left leg and hooks their inner left thigh. Your right arm let's go of the opponent's head and slides to the inside of their left arm. Now wrap your right arm around their back and reach toward the sky. Apply pressure on the opponent's left inner thigh with your right foot at the same time you reach for the sky. This will start the process of rolling the opponent over toward your left side. Once the opponent starts to lift off the ground, chop their right elbow out from underneath them with your left arm. This should be done at the same time you sweep the opponent's right knee out with your left leg. As you sweep the opponent's right knee and elbow, put your body weight onto your left shoulder and roll the opponent all the way over to your left side. Finish in the top mount position.

Abbreviated Directions:

From the headlock position, grab their right shoulder with your left hand. Pivot off their left hip and swing your hips out toward your right side. Circle your right leg around and hook the inside of their left thigh. Slide your right arm inside their left arm and reach upward with your right arm and leg. Chop their right elbow and leg out as you pivot on your left shoulder and roll over into top mount.

Fill In the Word:

F t h p, g t r s w y l h. P o t l h a s y h o t y r s. C y r l a a h t i o t l t. S y r a i t l a a r u w y r a a l. C t r e a l o a y p o y l s a r o i t m.

Linking Story:

A trapeze artist in tights is in my guard and she has me in a head lock with her right padlock arm. Her left leg is stretched out to my right side and the rest of her body weight is pressing down on me. My left hand turns into a bear trap that clamps down on her right shoulder as my chalk covered right hand holds her head down. Then my right leg turns into a swing and hangs from her left outstretched leg. I hold her head down with my right hand as I swing my hips out toward my right side. Once my hips have swung out to the right side, my right foot turns into a bailing hook and I hook the inside of her left thigh with it. Now I slide my chalk covered right hand inside her left arm and around her back. I start to lift up on my right bailing hook foot and reach toward the sky with my chalk cover right hand. Once the trapeze artist starts to lift off the ground, my left arm and leg turn into butcher knives that chop her right elbow and knee out from underneath her. I then pivot on my left shoulder that's on a balance beam as I roll her over and sit on a saddle that is cinched to her abdomen.

Fill In the Story:

Trapeze artist, padlock, bear trap, chalk, swing, bailing hook, chalk, bailing hook, knives, balance beam, and saddle.

Lesson 12-A: Elbow Escape – Top Mount – Standard Variation
(top of toilet room door)

Visual:

A person is leaning against a fire escape with their elbow while they sit on a horse at the top of the door. Then a bear shoots at the person with a shot gun but misses and hits the door.

Directions:

From the bottom of top mount, place your right hand on the opponent's back and hug them close to your body. Place your left leg flat on the ground. Keep your right leg bent with your right foot flat on the ground to pivot off of. Turn your hips onto your left side by bumping your hips up slightly and pivoting on your right foot. Now block the opponent's right knee with your left elbow or hand. Use your left elbow to raise the opponent's right knee off of the ground and slide your left knee north under their right leg. Return to your back and trap the opponent's right leg with your left leg. Hug the back of the opponent's neck with your left arm. Then block the opponent's right knee with your right elbow or hand. Push off their right knee and turn your hips onto your right side. Return to your back and bend your right knee toward the sky in front of the opponent's left thigh. Now switch arm positions behind the opponent's neck and establish stage one of the punch block series from a three-quarter guard position. Place your left leg loosely around the opponent's back. Then pivot off of your right foot as you swing your hips toward your right side. Swing your lower right leg around the opponent's left leg and return to your back. Cross your feet behind the opponent's back to establish a closed guard.

Abbreviated Directions:

From the bottom mount position, hug their back with your right arm and push their right knee south with your left elbow. Trap their right leg and hug their neck with your left arm. Push against their left knee and slide your right leg out. Establish stage one and swing your hips toward your right side. Finish by swinging your right leg around to their back and cross your legs.

Fill In the Word:

F t b m p, h t b w y r a a p t r k s w y l e. T t r l a h t n w y l a. P a t l k a s y r l o. E s o a s y h t y r s. F b s y r l a t t b a c y l.

Linking Story:

The opponent is mounted on top of me when my right hand turns into a bear's paw and digs into their back. My left leg turns into a heavy shot gun that lays flat on the ground. My right knee bends toward the sky like a teepee. At the base of the teepee is a ram which is also my right hip. This ram strikes its head against the opponent's left hip so that I can lie on my left side and press more weight on the shot gun. Now my left elbow turns into a banana, and it slips under the opponent's right knee while my left side shotgun leg bends in half and slides under my left side banana elbow. My left side shotgun leg now turns into a teepee that is hooked around the opponent's right leg. I now lie on my back and hug the back of the opponent's neck with my left arm that is coated in honey. Then I push against their left knee with my right bear paw in order to get onto my right side. Once I'm on my side I pull my right side teepee leg in front of the opponent's left thigh and stand it upright again. Now my other teepee leg turns into a bailing hook, and I loosely stick it into the opponent's back. I place my right bear paw arm behind the opponent's neck and use my left armpit that is a bear trap to trap the opponent's right arm down. I then plant my weight on my right foot that has grown roots into the ground and swing my hips toward my right side. Now my right leg turns into a bailing hook that I swing around the opponent's left leg. I then return to my back and cross my crucifix shaped legs behind their back.

Fill In the Story:

Bear paw, shotgun, teepee, ram, banana, shotgun, teepee, honey, bear paw, teepee, bailing hook, bear paw arm, bear trap, roots, swing, bailing hook, and crucifix.

Lesson 12-B: Hook Removal Variation (left side of toilet room door)

Visual:

A cheerleader with a hook arm is sitting on a fire escape on the left side of the door when she gets shot in the right ankle with a razor tipped arrow. She throws her hook arm at the shooter, and it knocks him out.

Directions:

If your legs are trapped by the opponent's leg hooks, extend your right leg straight out to the side and circle it around until its free. As you are lowering your right foot down to the ground place it on the heel of the opponent's right hook. When you press down on the opponent's right heel straighten your left leg. Lay your extended left leg down on top of your right foot that is still holding down the opponent's right ankle. Now you can slide your right foot out from underneath your extended left leg. Make sure you keep your extended left leg pressed firmly against the ground so that the opponent cannot re-hook your left leg. Finish with the standard variation from here now that you are free from the opponent's leg hooks.

Abbreviated Directions:

To unhook your right leg, extend it out toward your right side and circle it around. Place your right foot on their right heel. Lay your extended left leg on top of your right foot. Slide your right foot out and press your left leg onto the ground. Finish with the standard variation.

Fill In the word:

T u y r l, e i o t y r s a c i a. P y r f o t r h. L y e l l o t o y r f. S y r f o a p y l l o t g. F w t s v.

Linking Story:

The opponent has my legs hooked in top mount, so my right leg turns into an arrow with a razor-sharp tip as my foot. My right arrow leg extends straight out to the side and circles around to pierce the opponent's right ankle on the opposite side. Now my left leg extends and turns into a shot gun. I lay my left shotgun leg next to my right arrow tip foot before pulling the arrow tip out and replacing it with my left shotgun leg. I now press my left shotgun leg flat on the ground where it presses into the concrete because it's so heavy. I then complete the standard elbow escape variation from here.

Fill In the Story:

Arrow, arrow tip, shotgun, arrow tip, shotgun, and concrete.

Lesson 12-C: Fishhook Variation (right side of toilet room door)

Visual:

A cheerleader is hanging from a large fishhook that is hooked through the right side of the door.

Directions:

If you cannot turn your hips to the side in the standard variation, use your right foot to hook the opponent's right ankle. Push against the opponent's right knee with your left elbow or hand to make sure their right leg remains far enough south to hook. Now lift your right leg up at the same time you push their right knee up with your left elbow or hand. Immediately slide your left knee north under the opponent's right leg and hook their right leg with your left leg. Finish with the standard variation from here.

Abbreviated Directions:

Hook the opponent's right ankle with your right foot. Push against their right knee with your left elbow. Lift your right foot up and push their right leg over your left leg and trap it. Finish with the standard variation.

Fill In the Word:

H t o r a w y r f. P a t r k w y l e. L y r f u a p t r l o y l l a t i. F w t s v.

Linking Story:

The opponent is too heavy to bump their right hip up, so my right foot turns into a large fishhook. I then hook the opponent's right ankle with my right fishhook foot and lift up on it. Once I lift their right ankle up, my left elbow turns into a banana that I slip under their right knee so that my left knee can slide under my banana elbow. Once my left leg is free it turns into an upright teepee that I trap the opponent's right leg with. I now complete the standard elbow escape variation from here.

Fill In the Story:

Fishhook, banana, and teepee.

Lesson 12-D: Heel Drag Variation (bottom of toilet room door)

Visual:

A cheerleader drags her high heeled alligator skin shoe across the bottom of the door.

Directions:

If the opponent's right leg comes up light during the fishhook variation, slide your left knee up to prevent their right leg from falling back down to the ground. Now let go of the fishhook and wrap your right leg over the top of their right ankle to trap it with your calf and hamstring. After their right leg is trapped, place your right foot on the ground. Now lie flat on your back to lift the opponent's right knee off of the ground. Push the opponent's right knee south with your left hand and hook your left leg over their right leg to trap it in place. Finish with the standard variation from here.

Abbreviated Directions:

If their right leg is light, use your left knee to hold it up. Hook your right leg over their right ankle and lie flat on your back. Push their right leg south and trap it with your left leg. Finish with the standard variation.

Fill In the Word:

I t r l i l, u y l k t h i u. H y r l o t r a a l f o y b. P t r l s a t i w y l l. F w t s v.

Linking Story:

If the opponent's right leg is limp like a slippery fish, I slide my left knee up like a teepee to prevent it from falling back down. The back of my right leg turns into an alligator's mouth, and it clamps down on the opponent's slippery fish right leg. Now

I alligator roll to my back which forces the opponent's right knee to lift up. My left leg now turns into a teepee that traps the opponent's right fish leg. I now complete the standard elbow escape variation from here.

Fill In the Story:

Fish, teepee, alligator mouth, alligator roll, and teepee.

Lesson 13: Positional Control - Side Mount (left wall of shower)

Visual:

A woman is controlling a horse with reins as she sits sideways on its back and uses a compass on the left side of the shower wall.

Lesson 13-A: Bridge and Roll Prevention Variation (rear wall of shower)

Visual:

A Dallas Cowboy's cheerleader rolls a condom across a bridge on the rear wall of shower. Her left arm is frozen, and her right arm is on fire.

Directions:

From the right side of the opponent, place your left arm behind their neck and your right arm under their left armpit. Clasp your hands together behind the opponent's back with a thumbless gable grip. Stay heavy on the opponent by placing your chest directly in the center of their chest and keep your head low. Your left foot is planted on the ground north of the opponent's shoulder and your left knee is slightly bent. Your right leg is extended out to the side south of the opponent's right hip and your lower right hip is resting on the ground. If the opponent tries to roll toward you maintain chest pressure and your braced legs will prevent them from rolling. If the opponent tries to roll away from you, maintain chest pressure, unclasp your hands, remove your right hand that is under their left armpit, and brace out to their left side with it.

Abbreviated Directions:

From the opponent's right side, hug their neck with your left arm and place your right arm under their left armpit. Clasp your hands together with a thumbless grip. Extend your left leg north of their right shoulder and extend your right leg south of their right hip. Maintain chest pressure and brace with your right arm if needed.

Fill In the Word:

F t o r s, h t n w y l a a p y r a u t l a. C y h t w a t g. E y l l n o t r
s a e y r l s o t r h. M c p a b w y r a i n.

Linking Story:

From the right side of the opponent my northern left arm turns into a frozen popsicle that I place behind the opponent's neck. My southern right arm is on fire and it's under the opponent's left shoulder where it burns their armpit hair. I clasp my hands together and my thumbs start to melt off. An elephant steps down on my back and smashes my chest into the opponent's chest. My northern left knee has a brace filled with ice that keeps it slightly bent. My northern left foot turns into an icicle that melts into the ground north of the opponent's shoulder. My right leg is on fire and it's south of the opponent's hips. I try to put out the fire by pressing my right hip into the ground. If the opponent tries to roll away from me, my fiery right hand will turn into a shovel that digs into the ground.

Fill In the Story:

Popsicle, armpit hair, melting thumbs, elephant, ice knee brace, icicle foot, fire, and shovel.

Lesson 13-B: Guard Prevention Variation (right wall of shower)

Visual:

A British guard with a frozen left leg and a fiery right leg hands a condom to a Dallas Cowboy's cheerleader on the right side of the shower wall.

Directions:

If you feel the opponent pushing downward on your hip so they can slide their right leg out, you will need to immediately switch leg positions. You can switch your leg positions by sliding your southern right leg under your left leg until it is facing north along the side of the opponent. The opponent's right elbow should now be resting on top of your hip. If it's not, you can place it there by unclasping your hands and using your left hand that was under their neck to lift it up onto your hip. If the opponent tries to bridge and roll away from you, unclasp your hands and brace with your right arm that was under their left armpit. If the opponent tries to roll toward you, quickly switch back to your previous leg positions. You can alternate back and forth between the two leg positions as many times as you need to in order to prevent the opponent from rolling or putting you in their guard.

Abbreviated Directions:

From the right side mount position, switch your leg positions if the opponent pushes downward on your hips. Their right elbow should now rest on top of your lap. Brace with your right arm and switch your leg positions back if the opponent tries to roll away from you.

Fill In the Story:

F t r s m p, s y l p i t o p d o y h. T r e s n r o t o y l. B w y r a a s
y l p b i t o t t r a f y.

Linking Story:

If the opponent starts to push downward on my hip to escape, my fiery southern right leg will switch positions with my frozen northern left leg. The opponent's right elbow will then turn into a banana that will slide on top of my lap. If the opponent tries to roll away from me, my right fiery hand will dig into the ground like a shovel. I will then switch my legs back to their original position like I'm sprinting in the Olympics.

Fill In the Story:

Fiery right leg, frozen left leg, banana, shovel, and Olympics.

Lesson 13-C: **Mount Transition** (front wall of shower)

Visual:

A saddle is cinched around a train that is rolling across the front wall of the shower. A person grabs the horn of the saddle and digs their knees into the side of the train to hitch a free ride.

Directions:

From the right side mount position, pull both of your knees in next to the opponent. Slide your right southern shin across the opponent's abdomen and brace out with your right underhook arm. Place your head on the ground as you lower your right knee to the ground and slide it south. Now rotate your hips across the opponent as you swing your right shin off of their abdomen and onto the ground. Quickly slide both of your knees up under the opponent's armpits to secure a high mount position. If the opponent blocks your knees with their elbows, establish leg hooks instead.

Abbreviated Directions:

From the right side mount position, pull both of your knees in next to the opponent. Slide your right shin across their abdomen and brace with your right arm. Place your head on the ground as you lower your right knee onto the ground and slide it south. Swing your right shin off their abdomen and onto the ground. Finish by sliding your knees north into a high mount position.

Fill In the Word:

F t r s m p, p b o y k i n t t o. S y r s a t a a b w y r a. P y h o t g a y l y r k o t g a s i s. S y r s o t a a o t g. F b s y k n i a h m p.

Linking Story:

From the right side mount position, my northern left knee turns into a sharp icicle and I drive it into the right shoulder of the opponent. My southern right knee turns into a red-hot spear that I drive into the opponent's right hip. My frozen left knee starts to melt and run down my lower leg that is now pressed against the opponent's right side. My southern right knee catches my right shin on fire, so I place my shin on the opponent's abdomen to put it out. My fiery southern right arm has a shoulder brace on that is filled with ice that I place north of the opponent's left shoulder. I press my head and fiery right knee onto the ground to put it out. Once my fiery right knee touches the ground it turns into a match that I slide south to set it back on fire. My frozen northern left foot turns into a fence post and my hips turn into a tether ball that is attached to the post. I swing my tether ball hips across the opponent's abdomen which causes my fiery shin to swing over and crash onto the ground. I quickly slide both of my knees up into the opponent's armpits that are covered in glue. If the opponent blocks my knees with their elbows my legs turn into fishhooks that hook their legs.

Fill In the Story:

Icicle, spear, melting knee, fiery abdomen, iced shoulder, burning knee, match, fence post, tether ball, glue, and fishhooks.

Lesson 14: Body Fold Takedown (bathtub)

Visual:

A folded towel falls off the edge of the bathtub and two pistols fall out and go off.

Directions:

If the opponent throws a punch, kick, or is taking a step toward you with their left foot forward, shoot in with your hands up by your face and establish the clinch. To establish the clinch, your right leg should be to the outside of the opponent's front left leg. Your left leg should be out in front of the opponent's legs for base. Wrap your right arm behind their waist and grab your right wrist with your left hand in a thumbless grip. Stand tall with your chest and head pressed next to their chest and head. Do not push your hips away from the opponent. Your head needs to face the direction of your clinched hands. If your head changes direction, your hips must also change direction by straddling the opposite leg. Now lower your body and pull the opponent's waist into you. Lift up on their body and push your head and chest against them until they fall backwards onto the ground. On the way down to the ground bring your right leg forward and place it on the ground to help slow the fall. You also need to release your hand grip in midair so that you can use both arms to brace with as you land. As soon as you land on the ground in half mount you need to pull your left leg across the opponent's right thigh to establish full mount.

Abbreviated Directions:

From the clinch position, lower your body and squeeze their waist with your arms. Lift up on their body as you push them backward with your chest. Step forward with your right foot to slow the fall. Release your hand grip and brace with your arms. Finish by hooking their right leg to establish top mount.

Fill In the Word:

F t c p, l y b a s t w w y a. L u o t b a y p t b w y c. S f w y r f t s t f. R y h g a b w y a. F b h t r l t e t m.

Linking Story:

The opponent throws a punch at me, so my arms turn into two pistols that I use to protect my face with as I shoot into their chest. The opponent is wearing a steel toe boot on his front left foot. The inside of my right rear foot has a strong magnet on it that gets stuck to the outside of the opponent's left boot. My right pistol arm that is closest to the opponent's back wraps around the back of their waist. My other left pistol arm turns into a monkey arm that grabs the end of my right pistol barrel wrist with a thumbless grip. My body now stands tall like a bear, and I bury my chest and head into the honey covered chest of the opponent. I make sure that I'm always able to see the banana themed watch on my left monkey wrist. If I can't see the watch on my monkey hand, I move my hips and head to face the direction of the watch. I lower my body like a frog getting ready to jump and I pull the opponent's waist in by pulling on my pistol barrel arm. The gun goes off because I squeezed too hard, and it startled me enough to lift the opponent up before falling forward on their body. As I'm falling to the ground, I bring my right outside foot forward to slow the fall. My right outside foot is wearing a turtle shell for a shoe. I also extend both of my eagle wing arms out to brace with. I land on the opponent who is wearing a saddle, but I only have my right foot in the stirrups. I quickly pull my left leg across their right thigh and put my left foot in the stirrup to establish full mount.

Fill In the Story:

Pistols, steel toe boot, magnet, pistol, monkey grip, bear, honey, banana watch, frog, gunshot, turtle shell, eagle wings, saddle, and stirrup.

Lesson 15: Clinch with Conservative Opponent (bathroom window)

Visual:

An elephant clinches their trunk down on a yardstick that is holding a honeycomb at the top of the bathroom window.

Directions:

If the opponent is hesitant to punch or shoot in on you take a couple steps back. The distance you step back should be two arm lengths away from the opponent so that they cannot punch or kick you. You want to lure the opponent into following you backwards by making them think you are afraid or retreating. Make sure your legs are matching the opponent's stance. If their right leg is forward your right leg should be forward. If the opponent switches stances, you should switch stances to match them. This will help you shoot in with your forward leg and establish the clinch from the correct angle. Do not take more than four steps backward before you shoot in and establish the clinch. Wait for the opponent to step toward you or throw a punch before you shoot in on them. The opponent needs to be in motion toward you when you cover your face and shoot into their chest and establish the clinch. Once you commit to shooting into the opponent, you must drive all the way through to their chest and drive them backward as you establish the clinch. If the opponent does not follow you backward this is a good time to walk away from the fight. You do not want them to lure you into following them. This would allow the opponent to take advantage of your forward motion.

Abbreviated Directions:

Take up to four matching steps backward, to lure the opponent into lunging at you. When they lunge at you, block your face, and shoot in for the clinch. Walk away if they do not follow you.

Fill In the Word:

T u t f m s b, t l t o i l a y. W t l a y, b y f, a s i f t c. W a i t d n f y.

Linking Story:

The opponent is a scared bear who is afraid to get too close to me. I place a honeycomb on a yard stick that is taped to another yard stick. I slowly moon walk backwards trying to get the bear to follow me. Once the bear starts to follow me, I block my face with pistol arms and shoot in to establish the clinch.

Fill In the Story:

Bear, honeycomb, yard stick, moon walk, and pistol.

Lesson 16: Headlock Counters (top of left side bathroom mirror)

Visual:

A mannequin head has a large padlock around its neck and is sitting on a calculator on top of the left side mirror.

Lesson 16-A: Modified Mount (left side of left side mirror)

Visual:

A supermodel is riding a bull with a gorilla behind her back on the left side of the mirror.

Directions:

If the opponent starts to roll over to their left side with you in a headlock from the top mount position, establish the modified top mount. If the opponent is about to roll over toward their left side and get on their knees. Brace your arms out and pull the opponent toward you in a circular movement by pressing your right heel into their abdomen. As you press your right heel into the opponent's abdomen, slide your left knee up toward their head. Every time the opponent tries to get up, make another small circular pivot.

Abbreviated Directions:

From the modified mount position, brace with your arms and press your right heel into their abdomen as you slide your left knee up toward their head. If the opponent tries to roll over, press your right heel into their abdomen and make a small circular pivot.

Fill In the Word:

F t m m p, b w y a a p y r h i t a a y s y l k u t t h. I t o t t r o, p y r h i t a a m a s c p.

Linking Story:

A silverback gorilla is mounted on a super model, and she has the gorilla in a headlock. The model starts to turn to her left side, so the gorilla establishes a modified mount. He pushes his shovel hands into the ground and presses his right heel with a spur on it into her abdomen. Then the gorilla slams his left knee into the back of her head and shoulders which crushes a banana that was lying next to her head. The model tries to roll over but as soon as she does the gorilla digs his right heel with a spur on it into her abdomen and his left knee into her head like he's riding a bucking bull in a clockwise circle. If the model stays on her side, the gorilla can finish her with an armlock. If the model tries to roll over, the gorilla can take her back and finish her with a rear naked choke.

Fill In the Story:

Gorilla, model, shovels, spur, banana, bull, and clock.

Lesson 16-B: Rear Naked Choke Finish (bottom of left side mirror)

Visual:

A naked super model is getting choked from behind by a gorilla with a checkered flag at the bottom of the mirror.

Directions:

If the opponent lets go of the headlock and turns over to get up on their knees, sink both of your leg hooks into their legs but do not cross your feet. Your weight should now be entirely on your toes and hands as you rock your body backward. Stay as low on the opponent's back as possible to avoid getting shook off. If you touch the opponent's back as you slide south it may create friction that can slow the move down. Now place your left arm over the opponent's left shoulder as you place your right arm under their right armpit. Complete the over under grip by clinching your hands together and placing your head next to the right side of their head. You can now stick to the opponent and finish with a rear naked choke.

Abbreviated Directions:

If the opponent rolls over to their knees, establish leg hooks and rock backwards on your hands and toes. Establish an over under grip and finish with a rear naked choke.

Fill In the Word:

I t o r o t t k, e l h a r b o y h a t. E a o u g a f w a r n c.

Linking Story:

A silverback gorilla is mounted on a super model. The model rolls over onto her knees, so the gorilla's legs turn into large fish hooks that he hooks the model's legs with. The gorilla then balances on his shovel hands. His feet turn into small rocking chairs that he rocks back on before securing the over under grip like a baby monkey. The gorilla's right arm turns into a snake and wraps around the model's neck before biting the back of his left arm's tricep. His left hand turns into a banana that he slides behind the model's head. The gorilla arches backward with his furry silver back to finish the choke.

Fill In the Story:

Gorilla, model, fishhooks, shovels, rocking chairs, baby monkey, snake, banana, and silver back.

Lesson 16-C: Armlock Finish (right side of left side mirror)

Visual:

A mannequin arm with a checkered flag wrapped around it is handcuffed to a gorilla's neck on the right side of the mirror.

Directions:

If the opponent stays on their left side in your modified mount without trying to get up, create a frame by pressing the edge of your left forearm into the lower part of their neck. Grab your left wrist with your right hand and place all of your weight onto your left arm until the opponent experiences enough pain to let go of the headlock. As the opponent's headlock starts to loosen pull your head up to take out the slack. If the opponent won't release the headlock with the frame, you can punch their nose, or pull your head back to create enough space to slip your head out. If at any time during the act of implementing the frame the opponent raises their hips to roll you over, immediately release the frame, and brace with your hands. You will then need to circle with them in the modified mount before attempting the frame again. Once the opponent becomes exhausted from trying to roll you over, you can apply the frame on their neck again. It may take several circular movements before the opponent gives up. When the opponent releases the headlock, grab their right arm that was around your neck with your right southern hand, and trap it next to the northern left side of your neck. If the opponent's right arm is bent, hook it with your right arm instead of grabbing it. Press down on the right side of their head with your left hand and walk your right foot up next to their chest. Once your foot is in position lower your right knee and balance on the edge of your right foot. Pivot on their head by placing all of your weight on your left hand with your fingers facing the direction you want your legs to end up. It's now time to pivot your hips around to a ninety-degree angle. Keep your hips low and tight to the opponent's shoulder as you swing your left leg around their head. Do not drop your sit bones to the ground until your left leg is all the way into position. Now that you are perpendicular with the opponent, bend both of your knees toward the sky with your heels placed tightly against their body. Squeeze both knees together around their trapped right arm. Now grab the opponent's right wrist with both of your hands as you lean backwards toward the ground. Finish by pulling their right arm straight back toward your right southern shoulder as you elevate your hips.

Abbreviated Notes:

From the modified mount position, break their headlock with a left arm frame. Grab or hook their right arm and walk your right foot north. Lower your right knee and place your weight on your left hand that is on their head. Swing your left leg around their head and sit down. Pull their right wrist toward your right shoulder and finish by elevating your hips.

Fill In the Word:

F t m m p, b t h w a l a f. G o h t r a a w y r f n. L y r k a p y w o y l h t i o t h. S y l l a t h a s d. P t r w t y r s a f b e y h.

Linking Story:

From the modified mount position, the model still has the gorilla in a headlock. The gorilla's northern left arm turns into a metal picture frame that he presses into her neck. The gorilla then pushes down on the frame with his right hand until the model releases the head lock. If the model tries to roll over, the gorilla will let go of the picture frame and brace with his shovel hands. Now that the gorilla's head is free, his southern right arm turns into a fiery bailing hook that he uses to hook the model's top right arm. The gorilla uses his left hand to smash a whipped cream pie into the side of the model's face and balances his weight on the pie. The gorilla's right foot that is in front of the model's abdomen has a dog leash attached to it. His right foot starts to walk up towards the model's armpit and gets stuck to her armpit with gluey deodorant. The gorilla opens his right hip so wide that it breaks like a turkey wish bone. Now he swings his left leg around the model's head like a helicopter blade and places it next to his right foot. The gorilla now uses both of his bear trap hands to grab the model's wrist and extends her arm. The model holds her thumb up and asks to hitch a ride to the gorilla's southern shoulder. Once the model arrives at the gorilla's southern shoulder, she still wants to fight so he lifts his groin and cracks a walnut that is stuck to the back of her right elbow.

Fill In the Story:

Model, gorilla, frame, shovels, bailing hook, pie, dog leash, gluey deodorant, wish bone, helicopter blade, bear traps, hitch hiker, and walnut.

Lesson 17: Double Leg Takedown (left side bathroom sink)

Visual:

An ostrich with double barrel shot gun legs falls out of the left side bathroom sink.

Directions:

When the opponent lunges toward you, lower your body, and shoot in with your left shoulder under their waist. Your legs should match the opponent's stance and your head should be to the outside of their front left leg. Grab the back of the opponent's knees and pull them toward you with one of their legs on each side of you. Use your rear, right foot and left shoulder to drive them all the way down to the ground. Pass their guard by pinning their left leg down to the ground and swinging your legs around into the side mount position. If the opponent is closer than two arm lengths away, shoot in to complete the take down. If the opponent is further than two arm lengths away, take a couple steps backward to lure them into lunging at you, before shooting in to take them down.

Abbreviated Directions:

When the opponent lunges toward you, lower your body, and shoot in with your left shoulder under their waist. Grab the back of their knees and pull their legs to each side of you. Drive them down to the ground with your left shoulder and right foot. Push their left leg down and swing your legs around into the side mount position.

Fill In the Word:

W t o l t y, l y b, a s i w y l s u t w. G t b o t k a p t l t e s o y. D t d t t g w y l s a r f. P t l l d a s y l a i t s m p.

Linking Story:

The opponent is a huge ostrich with double barrel shotgun legs, and he is trying to peck my eyes out. I'm holding up a wooden yard stick to keep him away from me. I then smack his beak with the yard stick to create a distraction before I squat down like a frog and shoot in. My head is on the outside of the ostrich's front left side shotgun barrel knee. I have a magnet earing on my left ear that gets stuck to the metal shotgun leg. I then pull his shotgun knees toward me which folds the shotgun barrels open, and the shells fall out of the chambers. My back right foot turns into a bulldozer and the blade of the bulldozer turns into my left shoulder. I drive straight through the ostrich's legs until he is lying flat on the ground. I push down on the ostrich's left leg and swing both of my chain legs around into side mount.

Fill In the Story:

Ostrich, shotguns, yard stick, frog, magnet earring, shotgun shells, bulldozer, and chains.

Lesson 18: Headlock Escape 1 (top of left side sink cabinet)

Visual:

A human shaped *piñata* has their head locked to a fire escape on top of the left side sink cabinet.

Lesson 18-A: Scissor Choke Variation (left side of left side sink cabinet)

Visual:

A cheerleader is choking a human shaped *piñata* with a pair of scissors on the left side of the sink cabinet.

Directions:

If the opponent has you in a headlock on your right side, roll to your right side and face the opponent. Create a frame by pressing your top left forearm into the opponent's neck as you push against your left wrist with your right hand. With your frame fully extended, use your left foot that is flat on the ground to help scoot your hips away from the opponent, and north toward their head. Keep scooting with your hips until your knees are in line with the opponent's neck. Now swing your top left leg over the opponent's throat and cross your feet. Push away from the opponent's body until you end up perpendicular to them. Once you are in position, hold the opponent's right arm for control. Straighten your legs and body to finish the scissor choke.

Abbreviated Directions:

From the right side headlock position, roll to your right side and face the opponent. Create a frame with your left arm and scoot your hips north. Swing your left leg over their throat and cross your feet. Hold their right arm and push away from their body. Finish by straightening your legs and body.

Fill In the Word:

F t r s h p, r t y r s a f t o. C a f w y l a a s y h n. S y l l o t t a c y f. H t r a a p a f t b. F b s y l a b.

Linking Story:

The opponent is a human shaped piñata who has me in a headlock from the right side control position. I roll over a tootsie roll and onto my right side. My top left arm turns into a metal picture frame. I place my left picture frame forearm onto the piñata's neck and push against it with my right hand until the piñata's head moves back. A scooter made out of ice appears under my hips and my hips slide north until my knees are in line with the piñata's neck. My legs turn into scissor blades, and I swing my top left scissor blade leg across the piñata's throat. My right scissor blade leg is behind its neck, and I hold onto the piñata's right arm for control. I squeeze and straighten my scissor blade legs until the head of the piñata gets cut off and candy falls out.

Fill In the Story:

Piñata, tootsie roll, picture frame, scooter, scissor blades, and candy.

Lesson 18-B: Scissor Failure Variation (right side of left side sink cabinet)

Visual:

A cheerleader with a cheese covered right elbow tries to cut the right side of the sink cabinet with scissors and they break.

Directions:

If the opponent is not being affected by the scissor choke, lean onto your right elbow that is closest to the ground. Use your left arm to reach across the opponent's chest and grab the back of their left tricep or shoulder. Transition from your right elbow to your right hand and swing your top left leg behind your body. Now press your chest against the opponent's chest and swing your bottom right leg under your left leg. Sprawl both of your legs out and establish an over under grip to finish in the side mount position.

Abbreviated Directions:

Lean onto your right elbow and grab their left tricep with your left hand. Extend your right arm and swing your left leg behind your body. Press your chest on their chest and swing your right leg behind your body. Sprawl your legs out and establish an over under grip to finish in side mount.

Fill In the Word:

L o y r e a g t l t w y l h. E y r a a s y l l b y b. P y c o t c a s y r l b y b. S y l o a e a o u g t f i s m.

Linking Story:

If the scissor choke fails and I'm not able to cut the human piñata's head off, I lean onto my bottom right elbow that is covered in cheese and partially sit up. My left hand turns into a bear trap that I use to reach across the piñata's chest and clamp down on the back of its left tricep until honey starts to ooze out of it. Now I transition from my cheesy right elbow to my right hand, that is also covered in cheese. Then I swing my top left scissor blade leg behind me. Now I press my chest into the piñata like I'm trying to pop a balloon on its chest. I then swing my right scissor blade leg under my left leg until I'm sprawled out like an eagle in side mount. I finish by securing an the over under grip with my monkey arms to establish side mount.

Fill In the Story:

Cheesy elbow, bear trap, honey, cheesy hand, scissor blade, balloon, scissor blade, eagle, and monkey arms.

Lesson 18-C: Super Lock Variation (bottom of left side sink cabinet)

Visual:

Superman's left leg is made from a scissor blade, and he is handcuffed to a cheerleader at the bottom of the sink cabinet. His right arm is covered in cheese that is dripping down onto the cheerleader's hand.

Directions:

If you cannot break the opponent's headlock with a frame and scissor choke, lean onto your right elbow and swing your top left leg around behind you. Now pull your bottom right leg out from underneath their neck and pass it under your left leg. Go to your knees, with your left knee by the opponent's right shoulder, and your right knee behind their right hip. Brace your arms out on both sides of the opponent. Step your right leg over their right side and place your right foot in front of their abdomen to establish the modified mount position. Keep your hips low to create an effective counterweight. Once the modified mount is established, break the headlock with a left arm frame, or punch their nose.

Abbreviated Directions:

Lean onto your right elbow and swing your left leg behind you. Pull your right leg out and go to your knees. Brace with your arms and place your right foot in front of their abdomen. Keep your hips low and finish by breaking the headlock with a frame or strike.

Fill In the Word:

L o y r e a s y l l b y. P y r l o a g t y k. B w y a a p y r f i f o t a. K y h l a f b b t h w a f o s.

Linking Story:

If the human piñata will not release the headlock, I place all of my weight onto my cheesy right elbow and swing my top left scissor blade leg behind me. I then swing my bottom right scissor blade leg under my left scissor blade leg and go to my knees. My northern left knee has an icicle spike on it and my southern right knee has a red-hot spear tip on it. I dig my left knee into the piñata's right shoulder and my right knee into its right hip. I brace with both of my arms that have shovels for hands. My southern right knee starts to catch the piñata on fire, so I pull it out of its right hip and step over into the modified mount position. I'm wearing a weightlifting belt that has lead weights attached to it to keep my hips low and heavy. Now my left arm turns into a metal picture frame that I press down on the piñata's neck with until they release the headlock.

Fill In the Story:

Cheesy elbow, scissor blades, icicle, spear tip, shovels, fire, weighted belt, and picture frame.

Lesson 19-A: Straight Armlock – Guard (top of closet door)

Visual:

A person with an arrow stuck in their arm is handcuffed to a British guard at the top of the closet door. The person knocks the guards helmet off with their left hand.

Directions:

If the opponent places their hands on your neck or chest from stage one of the punch block series, hold down the back of their neck with your left hand and uncross your legs. Spin your upper body toward the opponent's left leg and hook it with your right arm. Remove your left hand from behind the opponent's neck and push your left forearm against their throat. If their head is already pulled back, grab their right wrist with your left hand. Now spin your hips around and lift them up so that you can hook the opponent's neck with your left leg. After you hook the opponent's neck, dig both of your heels into the opponent's back as you cross your legs. Remove your right arm that is hooked under the opponent's left leg and use both hands to grab their right wrist. Extend the opponent's right arm toward your southern right shoulder and keep their left thumb facing toward the sky. Finish the armlock by elevating your hips as you keep the opponent's left arm pinned to your right shoulder.

Abbreviated Directions:

With their arms extended from the stage one position, hook the back of their neck with your left hand and uncross your legs. Spin your body around and hook their left leg with your right arm. Push your left forearm against their throat and hook your left leg over it. Grab their right wrist with both hands and elevate your hips to finish the armlock.

Fill In the Word:

W t a e f t s o p, h t b o t n w y l h a u y l. S y b a a h t l l w y r a.
P y l f a t t a h y l l o i. G t r w w b h a e y h t f t a.

Linking Story:

From stage one of the punch block series the opponent who is a British guard gets their hands free and places them on my neck. I place my left hand around the back of their neck which causes their helmet to fall off. I then spin like a bottle to the right side and hook the British guard's left leg with my right arm that is a large fishhook. I remove my left hand from behind the guard's neck and place my left forearm full of sharp metal spikes into their throat and push their head back. Now I elevate my hips like an elevator and hook the opponent's neck with my northern left leg that is in the shape of a large bailing hook. I then cross my legs and dig both of my heels that have large spurs on them into the guards back. I release my fishhook right arm from the guard's left leg and use both of my hands that are now bear traps to grab the guard's right wrist. I extend the guard's right arm toward my southern right shoulder that is on fire. Then I elevate my hips and crack a walnut that is on the back of the guard's right elbow.

Fill In the Story:

British guard, helmet, bottle, fishhook, metal spikes, elevator, bailing hook, spurs, bear traps, fire, and walnut.

Lesson 19-B: Triangle Transition (bottom of closet door)

Visual:

A train with a large triangle on its roof is rolling across the bottom of the door. The triangle slides off the roof because it is covered in oil.

Directions:

If the opponent pulls their right arm out when you spin around for the armlock, keep your right leg pressed into their back. Now swing your left leg around to the other side of the opponent's neck and cross your feet behind their back. Let go of the opponent's left leg with your right arm and grab the opponent's left wrist with both hands. Then straighten your body and pull their left arm across your abdomen. If the opponent does not let you pull their left arm all the way across you can still finish the choke with their arm bent. You can also extend your hips upward to pull their arm across then lower your hips back down to hold their arm in place. Now remove your right hand from the opponent's left wrist and hook it behind their head. Pull down on the opponent's head as you hold their left wrist next to your left thigh. Finish with a standard triangle choke from here.

Abbreviated Directions:

If the opponent pulls their right arm out, swing your left leg around to the other side of their neck, and cross your feet. Grab their left arm with both hands and pull it across your waist as you straighten your body. Pull down on their head with your right hand and finish with a triangle choke.

Fill In the Word:

I t o p t r a o, s y l l a t t o s o t n, a c y f. G t l a w b h a p i a y w a y s y b. P d o t h w y r h a f w a t c.

Linking Story:

The British guard's right arm is coated in oil, so he is able to pull it away from me when I go for the armlock. I immediately press my southern right leg into the guard's back with a spur that is on fire. My northern left leg turns into a large frozen bailing hook that I swing around to the other side of the guard's neck and hook it into his back. Then I cross my southern leg with the burning spur over the frozen bailing hook and into the guard's back. I let go of the guard's left leg with my fishing hook right arm and grab the guard's left wrist that is between my legs with both of my bear trap hands and pull it across my body like a seat belt. I remove my right hand from the guard's left wrist and hook the back of their neck with my fishhook right hand. Now I pull down on the guard's head with my right fishhook hand and hold their left wrist next to my left thigh with my left bear trap hand. I uncross my feet from behind the guard and dig my right foot that has a spike under it into their left hip. Then I push against their left hip as I walk north on my shoulders. My shoulders have two frozen shoes attached to them. I walk my body north until my hips are directly under the guard's neck. Now I bend my left leg that is over their right shoulder tightly around the back of their neck. I have metal spikes on the back of my left calf that dig into the back of the guard's neck. Now I grab my left ankle with my right fishhook hand that was holding the back of the guard's head and use it to pull my left leg toward me. Then my right leg that is on the guard's left hip turns into a large padlock that locks down over my left ankle. Now both of my fishhook hands pull down on their head as I elevate my hips. I squeeze my knees together until tea flows out of his nostrils.

Fill In the Story:

British guard, oil, spur, bailing hook, bear traps, seat belt, fishhook, spike, frozen shoes, spikes, fish hook, padlock, fish hooks, and tea.

Lesson 20-A: Double Ankle Sweep - Knees on Chest (top of left side closet shelf)

Visual:

A person is kneeling down with spike covered knee pads dug into their chest as they sweep off their ankles with a broom on top of the left side closet shelf.

Directions:

If the opponent is standing over you from the closed guard position, grab their ankles with a thumbless grip at the same time you place your knees together on their chest. Let your feet rest on each side of their torso. Push your knees into the opponent's chest by thrusting your hips upward and pull their ankles toward you at the same time. Once the opponent is down, lean onto your bent right elbow. Now lean toward the opponent's head by pushing off of your right hand and extending your right elbow. As you sit up grab the back of the opponent's neck with your left hand and pull yourself all the way up into top mount.

Abbreviated Directions:

If the opponent is standing over you from the closed guard position, grab their ankles, and place your knees on their chest. Push your knees into their chest by elevating your hips and pulling on their ankles. Sit up with your right arm and hook the back of their neck with your left hand. Finish by pulling yourself into top mount.

Fill In the Word:

I t o i s o y f t c g p, g t a, a p y k o t c. P y k i t c b e y h a p o t a. S u w y r a a h t b o t n w y l h. F b p y i t m.

Linking Story:

A criminal is standing over me with an ankle monitor on. My arms turn into gorilla arms, and I grab the criminal's ankles with a thumbless grip and place my knees on their chest with spiked knee pads. The criminal has a pistol on each side of his waist, so I trap them with my feet. Now an airbag goes off under my hips which causes me to push my knee pad spikes into their chest. I also pull both of their ankles at the same time the airbag goes off. Once the criminal is down on the ground, I lean onto my cheese covered right elbow and extend my cheesy right arm until my hand is flat on the ground. I then hook the back of the criminal's head with my left hand that is in the shape of a bailing hook. I pull on the back of the criminal's head until I'm sitting on a saddle that is cinched to their waist.

Fill In the Story:

Criminal, ankle monitor, gorilla arms, spiked knee pads, pistols, airbag, cheese, bailing hook, and saddle.

APPENDIX: SAMPLE MIND MAP

Lesson 20-B: Kick Variation (bottom of left side closet)

Visual:

A cheerleader kicks her feet into an opponent's waist, and they go flying into the wall under the left side closet shelf.

Directions:

If the opponent is standing tall and you cannot reach their chest with your knees, place your feet on their waist. Once your feet are on the opponent's waist, grab their ankles with a thumbless grip. Now push your feet into the opponent's waist as you pull their ankles toward you. Stand up in base once the opponent is down on the ground. Now step around the opponent's legs by grabbing one of their ankles and pulling it across your body. Finish by establishing side mount. If the opponent tries to get up, immediately shoot in from the side and establish side mount.

Abbreviated Directions:

Place your feet on the opponent's waist and grab their ankles. Push your feet against their waist as you pull on their ankles to take them down. Stand up in base with your right arm and pull one of their ankles across your body. Finish by establishing side mount.

Fill In the Word:

P y f o t o w a g t a. P y f a t w a y p o t a t t t d. S u i b w y r a a p o o t a a y b. F b e s m.

Linking Story:

A criminal is standing up straight with arrows for legs and is wearing an ankle monitor. My knees cannot reach his chest, so I place my feet under his waist belt. My arms turn into gorilla arms, and I grab the criminal's ankles with a thumbless grip. An airbag goes off under my hips which causes my feet to explode into the criminal's waist. I pull both of their ankles at the same time the airbag goes off. Once the opponent is down on the ground, I stand up by folding in my right leg like a pocketknife and place my right arm into the ground like a shovel. My left leg forms a teepee that I push off of at the same time I balance on my shovel right hand. My folded pocketknife right leg extends open and the blade sticks into the ground behind my right hand. I now stand all the way up and my left arm turns into a yard stick to keep the criminal away. I then grab the criminal's ankle monitor and pull it across my body to establish side control. If the criminal tries to get up before I can grab their ankle monitor, I will shoot in from the side and crush their chest with my chest like an elephant is standing on my back. I will then secure an over under grip and maintain side control.

Fill In the Story:

Criminal, arrows, ankle monitor, belt, gorilla arms, airbag, folded knife, shovel, teepee, blade, yard stick, ankle monitor, and elephant.

Lesson 21: Pull Guard (rear left side closet)

Visual:

A British guard with a large magnet earing is sitting in a recliner on the rear left side of closet when he pulls the handle to kick up his feet.

Directions:

Position your head to one side of the opponent's head. Hook both of your arms under the opponent's armpits and place your hands on the back of their shoulders. Square your hips up with the opponent. Step or jump forward so that both of your feet are close to the opponent's feet. Squat down and shoot your hips back as you pull the opponent down to the ground. Hook your legs high around their back and cross your feet to establish a closed guard. Slide your underhooks out and pull the opponent's head down close to the side of your head with one arm. Wrap your other arm around their arm trapping it under your armpit. Finish by pressing your forearm that is trapping the opponent's arm into your thigh to prevent them from pulling their arm away and punching you.

Abbreviated Directions:

From a standing position, place your head next to their head and establish underhooks. Square your hips and step forward. Squat down and shoot your hips backward as you pull the opponent down to the ground. Cross your feet behind their back and finish by establishing stage one.

Fill In the Word:

F a s p, p y h n t t h a e u. S y h a s f. S d a s y h b a y p t o d t t g. C y f b t b a f b e s o.

Linking Story:

The opponent is wearing a magnet earring on their left ear that sticks to the left side of my head that is made from a metal plate. My arms turn into bailing hooks that I place under the opponent's armpits and stick into their shoulder blades. A square box is positioned between the opponent's hips and my hips. I jump forward and crush the cardboard box with my hips and my shoelaces get tied around the opponent's feet. Now I squat down, and a gun goes off that was in my back pocket. This causes my hips to shoot straight back dragging the opponent forcefully to the ground. My legs turn into large fishhooks that cross over each other and hook into the opponent's back. My arms now turn into large bananas that slip out from under the opponent's armpits and I establish stage one of the punch block series.

Fill In the Story:

Magnet earring, metal plate, bailing hooks, box, shoelaces, gunshot, fishhooks, and bananas.

Lesson 22-A: Headlock Escape 2 (top of built in cabinets)

Visual:

Two people have their heads padlocked to a fire escape on top of the built in cabinets. One person is eating a tootsie roll and the other person is eating cheese from under their armpit.

Directions:

If the headlock is too tight to create a frame, roll to your right side and tuck your right elbow in. Grab the opponent's left shoulder or bicep with your left hand and hook the inside of their top left leg with your left leg at the same time. Bend your right knee in and push off of your right foot until your hips are over the opponent. Now place your bent right knee onto the ground as you extend your right arm out for brace. Remove your left leg hook and place your left knee on the ground next to the left side of the opponent. Remove your left hand from the opponent's shoulder and place it on the ground to brace with. Place your body weight onto your hands and pull the opponent onto their left side. Tuck your right heel into the opponent's abdomen as you press your left knee into their bottom shoulder. From the modified mount position create a frame or punch the opponent in the nose to break the headlock.

Abbreviated Directions:

Roll onto your right side and tuck your right elbow in. Grab their left shoulder and hook their left leg. Push off your right foot until your hips are over the opponent. Place your right knee and hand on the ground. Then place your left knee and hand on the ground. Pull the opponent onto their left side and establish the modified mount. Break the headlock with a frame or strike.

Fill In the Word:

R o y r s a t y r e i. G t l s a h t l l. P o y r f u y h a o t o. P y r k a
h o t g. T p y l k a h o t g. P t o o t l s a e t m m. B t h w a f o s.

Linking Story:

The opponent has me in a tight headlock from the right side position. I roll over a large tootsie roll and face the opponent. My bottom right elbow tucks in squirting a packet of cheese out from under my right armpit. My top left hand turns into a bear trap and clamps down on the opponent's top left shoulder while my top left foot digs in a sharp spur into their top left leg. Now I bend my bottom right knee like a frog and push off the ground with my right webbed frog foot until my hips are over the opponent. Then I place my right frog knee onto the ground for base at the same time I extend my right arm out to brace with. My right arm has a red elbow brace on for support. Now I pull my spur out of the opponent's left leg and place my left frog knee onto the ground. I then release my left bear trap hand and place it out to brace with. The left arm also has a red elbow brace on it. From the back mount position, the opponent still has me in a head lock, so I pull the opponent backward like I'm a bulldozer in reverse with a loud beeping sound. Once the opponent is on their left side, I press my right heel that has a spur on it into their abdomen and sit on a saddle that is cinched to their right side to secure the modified mount position. I finish the escape by pressing my left picture frame forearm into their neck until they let go.

Fill In the Story:

Tootsie roll, cheese, bear trap, spur, frog foot, frog knee, elbow brace, spur, frog knee, elbow brace, bulldozer, spur, saddle, and picture frame.

Lesson 22-B: Super Base Variation (left side of built in cabinets)

Visual:

Superman is standing on a baseball base with his hands in a V formation on the left side of the cabinets. He has a large spear tip on his left shoulder.

Directions:

If the opponent has their legs spread out and you cannot roll them over into a modified mount, extend your left arm backwards and place the point of your left shoulder into the muscle on the side of their spine. Place all of your weight onto your head by standing on your feet and balancing with your braced right hand. In one sudden movement shift all of your body weight from your head onto your left shoulder that is pressed into the opponent's back. Use the right hand that you were bracing with to pull the opponent's right hand off of your neck. This will break the headlock and you can now transition into a modified mount or take their back if they try to get up.

Abbreviated Directions:

If their legs are too wide to pull them into a modified mount, place the point of your left shoulder into the right side of their spine. Place your weight onto your head, then shift your weight onto your left shoulder. Pull their right arm off your neck with your right hand. Finish by transitioning into a modified mount or take their back.

Fill In the Word:

I t l a t w t p t i a m m, p t p o y l s i t r s o t s. P y w o y h, t s y w o y l s. P t r a o y n w y r h. F b t i a m m o t t b.

Linking Story:

If the opponent's legs are spread too far apart to secure the modified mount, I will place the spear tip of my left shoulder into the muscle on the side of their spine. Now I place all of my body weight onto my head which turns into a shovel that digs into the ground. I keep my shovel head pressed into the ground by standing on my webbed frog feet and balancing with my braced right arm that has a red elbow brace on it. In one sudden movement my shovel head releases to the side and all of my body weight crashes down on my spear tip left shoulder. The spear tip goes all the way through the opponent, and I use my right bear trap hand to pull their arm off of my neck. I now sit on a saddle that cinched to their side or back.

Fill In the Story:

Spear tip, shovel head, frog feet, elbow brace, spear tip, bear trap, and saddle.

Lesson 22-C: Punch Block Variation (right side of built in cabinets)

Visual:

A cheerleader is punching a cinder block with a bear trap on her right hand on the right side of the cabinets.

Directions:

If you are in a headlock from the right side position and the opponent is getting ready to punch you, grab their left punching arm by the wrist with your bottom right hand and push it back away from you. Now take your left arm that is behind their back and reach under the opponent's top left armpit and hook their left forearm with a thumbless grip. Both hands are now holding the opponent's left arm. From this position you can hook the opponent's left leg with your left leg and complete the standard variation. Once you have transitioned to their back with your head still in a headlock let go of the opponent's left arm and brace with both hands. Transition into a modified mount and finish by breaking their headlock with a frame or strike.

Abbreviated Directions:

From the right side headlock position, grab their left punching wrist with your right hand and push it backward. Hook their left forearm with your left hand and hook their left leg with your left leg. Brace with both arms and finish with the standard variation.

Fill In the Word:

F t r s h p, g t l p w w y r h a p i b. H t l f w y l h a h t l l w y l l. B w b a a f w t s v.

Linking Story:

Mike Tyson has me in a head lock from the right side position and his left fist is pulled back ready to punch me in the face. My bottom right hand turns into a bear trap that clamps down on his left wrist. I push his left wrist backward like a bulldozer as it makes a beeping sound. My left arm slides under his left armpit that has a banana underneath it. I then hook his left forearm with my left bailing hook hand using a thumbless grip. I swing my hips over his back like a tetherball, and let go of his left arm, so that I can brace with my shovel arms. I pull him into a modified mount and sit on a saddle that is cinched to his right side. I finish by breaking the headlock with my left metal picture frame forearm.

Fill In the Story:

Mike Tyson, bear trap, bulldozer, banana, bailing hook, tetherball, shovels, saddle, and picture frame.

Lesson 23: Guillotine Choke (right rear side of closet)

Visual:

A guillotine blade is choking a football player on the right rear side of the closet.

Directions:

If the opponent shoots in on you, start by placing your hands on their shoulders as they push toward you. Now push the opponent's head to the right side of your body. Skip this step if the opponent's head is already on the side of your body because they shot in to take you down. Wrap your right arm under the opponent's neck. Grab your right wrist with your left hand using a thumbless grip. Keep your hips and legs back away from the opponent as you wrap your right arm as tight as possible around their neck. Once you have fully sunk in the choke step toward the opponent with both of your legs in a strong base. Lower your right armpit onto the back of the opponent's head while you pull up on your right forearm to finish the choke. If the opponent does not tap or pass out while standing. Pull guard with their head in the guillotine choke. Cross your legs high on their back and squeeze your legs together. Push the opponent south with your legs while you lower your right armpit and raise your right forearm to finish the choke.

Abbreviated Directions:

If the opponent shoots in on you, place your hands on their shoulders. Then push their head to your right side. Wrap your right arm around their neck and grab your right wrist with your left hand. Keep your hips back as you tighten the choke, then step forward to finish the choke. If they do not tap out, pull guard, and extend your crossed legs to finish the choke.

Fill In the Word:

I t o s i o y, p y h o t s. T p t h t y r s. W y r a a t n a g y r w w y l h. K y h b a y t t c, t s f t f t c. I t d n t o, p g, a e y c l t f t c.

Linking Story:

The opponent is wearing football shoulder pads and shoots in on me. I push against their shoulder pads before pushing their football helmet under my right armpit that is covered in glue. My right forearm turns into a large butcher knife, and I place it under the chin guard of their helmet. Now my left arm turns into a monkey's arm and grabs the dull side of the knife blade with a thumbless grip. A large beach ball is keeping my hips away from his hips. All of a sudden, the ball pops and both of my legs step toward the opponent in a strong base. My right armpit has steam coming out of it as I push down on the opponent's helmet and up on the butcher knife at the same time. If the football player does not tap out while standing, he turns into a British guard, and I pull him down into my guard with his head still in my guillotine. Once we are down on the ground, I cross my bailing hook legs and stick them into his back. I keep pressure on the choke by extending my legs south until steam comes out of his neck.

Fill In the Story:

Shoulder pads, helmet, glue, butcher knife, monkey, blade, beach ball, steam, blade, British guard, bailing hooks, and steam.

Lesson 24: Shrimp Escape (top of right side closet)

Visual:

A shrimp is crawling down a fire escape from the top of the right side of the closet.

Lesson 24-A: Block and Shoot Variation (left side of right side closet)

Visual:

A cheerleader with spear tips on her palms shoots a concrete cinderblock with a shotgun on the left side of the right side closet.

Directions:

If the opponent shoots in from your right side, roll to your right side and extend your arms. Place your bottom right hand on the opponent's hip and your top left hand on their chest. Use the forward momentum of the opponent pushing on you to spin your hips under the opponent. As your hips spin around slide your bottom right shin across their abdomen. Your bottom right ankle should hook the right side of the opponent's waist to keep from spinning too far. As your right shin slides into place, hook your top left leg behind their back. If the opponent is not pushing on you, grab onto their body or clothing to help you spin into position. Hold the opponent's head down on your torso with your left arm and use your right arm to block punches with. Push your right knee into their left hip and straighten your body away from the opponent. Now place your trapped right foot on the ground and swing your hips toward your right foot. Circle your right leg around the opponent's left leg and hook it behind their back. Finish by crossing your feet to establish a closed guard.

Abbreviated Directions:

From the right side position, extend your arms, and spin under the opponent with your left leg behind their back. Hold their head down and block punches with your right arm. Extend your body and place your right foot on the ground. Swing your hips toward your right foot and swing your right leg around their left leg. Finish by crossing your legs to establish a closed guard.

Fill In the Word:

F t r s p, e y a, a s u t o w y l l b t b. H t h d a b p w y r a. E y b a p y r f o t g. S y h t y r f a s y r l a t l l. F b c y l t e a c g.

Linking Story:

The opponent passes my guard and shoots in from the side, so I roll over a tootsie roll and face them. My bottom hand has a red-hot spear tip on the palm and my top hand has an ice pick on the palm. I extend both of my arms with my bottom red-hot spear tip hand sticking into the opponent's hip and my ice pick hand sticking into their chest. The opponent has iron weights attached to their back that is pressing their weight into my hands. I use their weight to spin my hips under the opponent like a spinning bottle. My shin turns into a banana that slides across the opponent's stomach with the hook of the peel snagging on their waist to prevent me from spinning too far. At the same time my banana shin is sliding across the opponent's stomach my top leg turns into a bailing hook and digs into their back. I hold down the opponent's head with one hand that is covered in glue and my other hand has an oversized boxing glove on to block punches. My knee that is trapped grows a unicorn horn that I stick into the opponent's left hip to push it away. Now my unicorn knee turns into a teepee and my foot rests flat on the ground. I then take my bailing hook leg out of the opponent's back which causes an airbag to go off that shoots my teepee side hip out to the side. Now my teepee leg turns into a tether ball that wraps around the opponent's leg. I cross my feet that are now bailing hooks and stick them into the opponent's back. I finish by establishing stage one of the punch block series.

Fill In the Story:

Tootsie roll, spear tip, ice pick, weights, bottle, banana, peel hook, bailing hook, glue, boxing glove, horn, teepee, airbag, tether ball, and bailing hooks.

Lesson 24-B: Shrimp and Shoot Variation (right side of right side closet)

Visual:

A cheerleader with spikes on her forearms shoots a shrimp with a shotgun on the right side of the right side closet.

Directions:

If the opponent gets past your hands and ends up chest on chest in side control, place one forearm on their hip and press your other forearm into their throat. Now push off their hip with your forearm and shrimp your hips away from the opponent. This will give you enough room to spin your hips under the opponent while sliding your shin across their stomach. You can now establish guard using the rest of the steps in the standard block and shoot variation.

Abbreviated Directions:

From the right side chest on chest position, place your right forearm on their hip and your left forearm on their throat. Shrimp your hips out, then spin under the opponent. Your right shin is across their abdomen and your left leg is across their back. Finish with the standard variation.

Fill In the Word:

F t r s c o c p, p y r f o t h a y l f o t t. S y h o, t s u t o. Y r s i a t a a y l l i a t b. F w t s v.

Linking Story:

If the opponent ends up with their elephant chest on my chest from the right side position, my right southern forearm will grow fiery metal spikes that I will stick into their hip. My left northern forearm will turn into solid ice and I will push the opponent's neck backward with it. Now I will push against the opponent's hip with my fiery forearm until it triggers an airbag under my hip that shoots my hips away from the opponent's hips. I now have enough room to spin my banana shin under the opponent's abdomen like a spinning bottle. I then complete the standard shrimp escape variation.

Fill In the Story:

Elephant, spikes, ice, airbag, banana, and bottle.

Lesson 24-C: Punch Block Variation (bottom of right side closet)

Visual:

A cheerleader punches a cinder block at the bottom of the right side of closet.

Directions:

If the opponent is strong enough to prevent you from shrimping your hips out toward your left side, pull their head in next to your head with your left arm. Now trap their left arm with your right arm to prevent them from punching you. Stay in this safe position until the opponent gets frustrated enough to try and stand up or they pull their body back to punch you. When the opponent pulls their body back, hold onto the back of their head with your left hand and use your right hand to push against their hip. This will give you enough room to shrimp out toward your left side. Now you have enough room to spin your body underneath them and slide your right shin across their abdomen. Finish with the standard variation from here.

Abbreviated Directions:

If you cannot shrimp out toward your left side, pull their head next to your head with your left arm, and trap their left arm with your right arm. Hold onto their head when they pull back, and push against their left hip to shrimp your hips out. Spin underneath the opponent and finish with the standard variation.

Fill In the word:

I y c s o t y l s, p t h n t y h w y l a, a t t l a w y r a. H o t h w t p b, a p a t l h t s y h o. S u t o a f w t s v.

Linking Story:

A five-hundred-pound silverback gorilla has me in side control. He is holding me so tight that I can't scoot my hips out to the side. One of my arms is covered in glue so I wrap it around the back of his neck. My other arm has a bear trap under my armpit that I use to clamp down on the gorillas punching arm. The gorilla gets mad and lets out a loud roar before pulling his body back like a bulldozer away from me. My glue covered arm is still holding onto the back of his neck but my other arm lets go of his punching arm and presses a metal spike into his hip. A scooter appears under my hip and I shrimp my hips out to the side. Now I spin like a bottle and place my banana shin across his abdomen and finish with the standard variation.

Fill In the Story:

Gorilla, glue, bear trap, bulldozer, spike, scooter, bottle, and banana.

Lesson 25-A: Kimura Armlock (top of right side mirror)

Visual:

A silk kimono is wrapped around a gorilla's arm that is locked to the top of the mirror by a metal bear trap.

Directions:

From the bottom of guard, grab the opponent's right wrist with your left hand. Uncross your legs and post off of your right foot. Lean onto your left elbow and sit up. As you lean onto your left elbow, swing your hips toward your right side. Now wrap your right arm around the backside of the opponent's right tricep and grab the frontside of your left wrist with a thumbless grip. If you can't reach your left wrist, slide your left wrist higher up on the opponent's arm, or lower your right arm down until you can reach it. Then push off both of your feet and lie flat on your back with both shoulders touching the ground. Keep the opponent's trapped right arm pinned to your chest as you pullback. Trap the opponent's right leg with your left leg if they are lying on top of you. If the opponent is on their knees hook your left leg around their back. Once the opponent's right leg is trapped or your left leg hook is in place, swing your hips out toward your left side and face the opponent. From this angle you will be able to cross your feet and trap the opponent's body in place. Keep the opponent's right arm pinned to your chest at a ninety-degree angle as you slowly twist their arm north. Use your back to create the twisting motion instead of your arms.

Abbreviated Directions:

From the bottom of guard, grab their right wrist with your left hand, then wrap your right arm behind their right arm and grab your left wrist. Push off your feet and lie flat on your back. Hook their right leg with your left leg and turn onto your left side. Cross your legs behind their back and finish by twisting their right arm north.

Fill In the Word:

F t b o g, g t r w w y l h, t w y r a b t r a a g y l w. P o y f a l f o y b. H t r l w y l l a t o y l s. C y l b t b a f b t t r a n.

Linking Story:

The opponent is in my guard. My left hand turns into a bear trap that clamps down on the British guard's right wrist. When I uncross my legs, they turn into teepee's, and I place both of my feet flat on the ground. I then lean onto my left cheese covered elbow that is on the same side as my bear trap hand and sit up. When I start to sit up an airbag goes off underneath me and it shoots my hips out to the right side. My right arm turns into a monkey's arm that I use to reach around the back of the opponent's right arm with. Then my right hand grabs my own left wrist with a thumbless grip. Our joined arms now turn into a metal picture frame. I keep the picture frame tight to my chest as I push against my teepee feet and pull the opponent north towards me. My shoulder blades turn into shovels that dig into the ground as I land. Now my left side teepee leg hooks around their right leg. If the opponent is on their knees my left teepee leg will turn into a bailing hook and dig into their back. A scooter then appears under my hips, and I scoot out toward the left side of the opponent's trapped arm. Now my legs turn into scissor blades that cross behind the opponent's back. The opponent's trapped right arm turns into a large pretzel that I twist at a ninety-degree angle using my gorilla back muscles.

Fill In the Story:

Bear trap, teepee, cheese, airbag, monkey, picture frame, teepee, shovels, teepee, bailing hook, scooter, scissors, pretzel, and gorilla.

Lesson 25-B: Rider Variation (left side of right side mirror)

Visual:

A cheerleader's right hand is glued to the throttle as she rides a motorcycle on the left side of the mirror.

Directions:

From stage one of the punch block series hold onto the back of the opponent's head with your right hand as they pull back. As the opponent pulls back, uncross your legs and post off of your right foot. Lean onto your left elbow and swing your hips toward your right side. Now wrap your right arm around the backside of the opponent's right tricep. Then grab the opponent's right wrist with your left hand. Finish the frame by grabbing the front side of your left wrist that is holding the opponent's right wrist. In order to prevent the opponent from pulling their arm away, you must grab their right wrist at the same time you are grabbing your left wrist. Follow the rest of the steps in the standard variation to complete the technique.

Abbreviated Directions:

From stage one, hold the back of their head with your right hand as they pull back. Uncross your legs and trap their right arm with a frame. Finish with the standard variation.

Fill In the Word:

F s o, h t b o t h w y r h a t p b. U y l a t t r a w a f. F w t s v.

Linking Story:

The opponent is wearing boxing gloves from stage one of the punch block series, I hold onto the back of the opponent's head with my right glue covered hand as they pull backward like a beeping bulldozer. As the opponent pulls back, I uncross my legs and post off of my right leg that is in the shape of a teepee. Then I lean onto my cheese covered left elbow and an airbag goes off under my hips that swings my hips toward the right side. I unhook my sticky right hand from behind the opponent's head and wrap it around the back of their right tricep like an anaconda snake. My left arm has a bear trap hand that clamps down on the opponent's right wrist. Now I bite my left wrist with my right anaconda snake hand and our arms turn into a metal picture frame. I then complete the standard variation.

Fill In the Story:

Boxing gloves, glue, bulldozer, teepee, cheese, airbag, snake, bear trap, snake bite, and picture frame.

Lesson 25-C: Forced Variation (right side of right side mirror)

Visual:

A cheerleader is playing an accordion in the bed of a Ford truck that is driving down the right side of the mirror.

Directions:

If the opponent does not pull back during stage one of the punch block series, use your leg hooks to push them south. Now push the opponent's head under your right armpit with your left hand. Uncross your legs and post on your right foot. Then swing your hips toward the right side and lean onto your left elbow. Finish by trapping the opponent's right arm with a frame and complete the standard variation from here.

Abbreviated Directions:

If the opponent does not pull back, use your legs to push them south. Push their head under your right armpit and post off your right foot. Swing your hips toward your right side and lean onto your left elbow. Trap their right arm with a frame and finish with the standard variation.

Fill In the word:

I t o d n p b, u y l h t p t s. P t h u y r a a p o y r f. S y h t y r s a l o y l e. T t r a w a f a f w t s v.

Linking Story:

If the opponent who is wearing boxing gloves does not pull back from stage one of the punch block series, I will use my legs to push them downward like I'm stretching an accordion. Now I will smash a whip cream pie into the right side of the opponent's head using my left hand. Once the opponent's head is on the right side of my body, I will place their head under my right armpit that is in the shape of a metal bear trap. Then I will post my right foot into the ground like a shovel and swing my hips toward the right side like a tether ball. Now I will lean onto my cheese covered left elbow and trap the opponent's right arm like a picture frame. Then I will finish with the rest of the standard variation steps.

Fill In the Story:

Boxing gloves, accordion, pie, bear trap, shovel, tether ball, cheese, and picture frame.

Lesson 26: Standing Headlock Defense (right side sink)

Visual:

A football player is standing in the right side sink with a padlock around his neck. His left arm is a bailing hook, and his right arm is a spear.

Directions:

If you are standing behind the opponent, and they have you in a head lock on the right side of their body, hook their left hip with your left hand that is behind their back. Reach your right arm across and place your right hand on their left thigh. Take a small step with your left foot to get closer to the opponent's right foot. Your left foot is now on the outside of the opponent's right foot with your toes facing toward their right heel. Now step squarely in front of the opponent with your right leg. Place your right foot on the inside of the opponent's left foot with your toes facing their left heel. Now keep your right arm braced on their left thigh, as you pull on their left hip, and sit down. As you are falling to the ground, pull the opponent over your left leg. Roll all the way over on top of the opponent and establish a modified mount. You can swing your right leg over the opponent's abdomen while you are rolling, or after you have stopped. Finish by breaking their headlock with a frame or strike.

Abbreviated Directions:

From the rear right side standing headlock position, hook their left hip with your left hand. Place your right hand on their left thigh and step in front of the opponent with your right foot. Hold onto their hip and sit down as you pull them over your left leg. Roll on top of their body and establish a modified mount. Finish by breaking their headlock with a frame or strike.

Fill In the Word:

F t r r s s h p, h t l h w y l h. P y r h o t l t a s i f o t o w y r f. H o t h a s d a y p t o y l l. R o t o t b a e a m m. F b b t h w a f o s.

Linking Story:

The opponent has me in a headlock on their right rear side while we are both standing. Their right arm is in the shape of a padlock. My left arm that is behind the opponent turns into a bailing hook that hooks their left hip. My right arm turns into a spear and stretches across the front of their body and sticks into their right thigh. My rear left foot gets tied to the outside of the opponent's right foot with my shoelace. My left toes have small flashlights on them that are shining on the opponent's right heel. Now I step forward with my right foot and it gets tied with my shoelace to the inside of the opponent's left foot. My right toes are also shining a light on their left heel as well. Now with my left bailing hook hand around the opponent's left hip and my right spear hand dug into their left leg, I sit down on a cushion and pull the opponent over my left leg. We crush a large dinner roll that is on the ground as I roll over on top of them. I establish a modified mount by sitting on a saddle that is cinched to their right side. My left arm then turns into a metal picture frame that I smash into the right side of the opponent's neck to escape the headlock.

Fill In the Story:

Padlock, bailing hook, spear, shoelace, flashlights, shoelace, flashlights, cushion, dinner roll, saddle, and picture frame.

Lesson 27-A: Punch Block Series - Stage 5 (top of right side sink cabinet)

Visual:

A stagecoach has five horses hitched to it and is carrying a cinderblock that has a boxing glove on top of it with a baseball bat below it on top of the right side sink cabinet. The stage coach is attacked by people who are shooting arrows at the driver's knees.

Directions:

If the opponent is not leaning on you, push them away by kicking at their knees. Once the opponent is out of your kicking distance keep your body centered with their body by pivoting off of one leg. One of your legs should be bent with your foot flat on the ground while your other leg is cocked back ready to strike. Your foot that is flat on the ground is the one you will use to turn with. You want to turn with the leg that is on the same side as the direction the opponent is moving. Keep your head and shoulders raised off of the ground to help pivot. Stand up in base if the opponent backs far enough away. If the opponent dives toward you, place both of your feet on their waist. Finish by blocking your face as you lower them down into stage one with your legs.

Abbreviated Directions:

From your back, push the opponent away and kick at their knees. Stay centered with their body by pivoting on your foot that is on the same side as the direction they are moving. Keep your other leg cocked back to strike. Stand up in base if you have enough room or place your feet on their waist if they dive toward you. Block your face and lower them down into stage one.

Fill In the Word:

F y b, p t o a a k a t k. S c w t b b p o y f t i o t s s a t d t a m. K y o l c b t s. S u i b i y h e r o p y f o t w i t d t y. B y f a l t d i s o.

Linking Story:

If the opponent is not putting weight on my feet like in stage four of the punch block series my legs will turn into arrows and I'll stick the arrows into the opponent's knees. The opponent's knees are wearing braces with a bullseye painted on them. I keep my body straight as an arrow with the opponent. If the opponent moves to one direction, my leg that is closest to the direction they are moving turns into a teepee, and I pivot off of it in order to stay straight with them. My other leg stays cocked back like a cobra snake that is about to strike. I then pivot on my back in whatever direction the opponent moves in like a water sprinkler. When the opponent steps back, I stand up on a baseball base. If they lean toward me, I block my face with boxing gloves and lower them down into stage one of the punch block series.

Fill In the Story:

Arrows, bullseye, teepee, cobra, sprinkler, base, and boxing gloves.

Lesson 27-B: Rollover Technique (bottom of right side sink cabinet)

Visual:

A person wearing black framed glasses is rolling over a beer bottle at the bottom of the sink cabinet.

Directions:

If the opponent grabs one of your ankles and pulls it across their body, keep your leg that is being pulled bent and stiff so that your entire body spins when they pull your leg. As you start to spin, roll toward the opponent, and place your free foot on their waist. Block your face from punches as the opponent leans forward onto your foot that is on their waist. If the opponent doesn't lean forward, kick at their knees, and resume the standard variation of stage five. Once the opponent is leaning forward, place your foot that they were holding on their waist. Now center your body with the opponent so that you can establish stage four of the punch block series. Finish by lowering the opponent down into stage one.

Abbreviated Directions:

If the opponent pulls your ankle and spins your body, roll toward their body and place your free foot on their waist. Now place your trapped foot on their waist and establish stage four. Finish by blocking your face as you lower them down into stage one.

Fill In the Word:

I t o p y a a s y b, r t t b a p y f f o t w. N p y t f o t w a e s f. F b b y f a y l t d i s o.

Linking Story:

I'm lying on my back on top of a beer bottle when the opponent pulls one of my ankles across their body. I keep my leg stiff like a metal fence post so that my body spins on the bottle. As my body starts to spin my free foot turns into a spear that extends over my trapped metal leg and sticks into the opponent's waist. Now I pull back my trapped foot that also turns into a spear and I stick it into the opponent's waist. I finish by repositioning my body to be straight as an arrow with the opponent and resume stage four of the punch block series. I finish by blocking my face with boxing gloves as I lower them down into stage one.

Fill In the Story:

Bottle, fence post, free spear, trapped spear, arrow, and boxing gloves.

Lesson 28-A: Hook Sweep (top of right side bathroom door)

Visual:

A person with a hook arm sweeps the top of the bathroom door with frog feet stuck to their waist.

Directions:

If the opponent is standing with their left leg forward, place your feet on the opponent's waist and hook the back of their left ankle with your right hand. Your knees must be bent in order to have room to straighten them to complete the sweep. If your legs are too straight walk your hips closer to the opponent. Now remove your left foot from the opponent's waist and hook it behind their right knee. Then extend your right leg that is on the opponent's waist. Pull the opponent's left ankle north as you retract your left leg hook behind their right knee. Your right leg must be extended before their left ankle will be light enough to pull. Finish by standing up in base once the opponent is down on the ground.

Abbreviated Directions:

With the opponent's left foot forward, place your feet on their waist and hook their left ankle with your right hand. Hook your left foot behind their right knee. Push your right foot against their waist as you pull on their left ankle and right knee to take them down. Finish by standing up in base.

Fill In the Word:

W t o l f f, p y f o t w a h t l a w y r h. H y l f b t r k. P y r f a t w a y p o t l a a r k t t t d. F b s u i b.

Linking Story:

My legs are bent like a frog and my webbed frog feet are stuck to the opponent's waist with glue. The opponent has their left leg forward so my right hand turns into a monkey hand and hooks their left ankle with a thumbless grip. I then remove my left frog leg from the opponent's waist. The left frog leg grows a fishhook foot that hooks behind the opponent's right knee. I complete the sweep by extending my right frog leg that's on the opponent's waist until their left ankle that is covered in feathers is light enough to pull. Once the ankle starts to move north, I retract my left fishhook frog foot at the same time I'm pushing against the opponent's waist and pulling their ankle. The opponent falls down and dust flies up. I finish by standing up on top of a baseball base.

Fill In the Story:

Frog feet, glue, monkey, fishhook foot, frog leg, feathers, fish hook foot, dust, and base.

Lesson 28-B: Sweep Follow Up (bottom of right side bathroom door)

Visual:

A broom follows a dirty pocket knife up the bathroom door.

Directions:

Make sure you push the opponent far enough away during the sweep that they do not fall down on top of you. Then roll onto your right elbow and bend your right leg under your left upright knee. Now sit up by extending your right arm and planting your right hand on the ground. Place your weight onto your right hand and push off your left foot so that you can swing your right leg behind your planted right hand. Extend your left arm toward the opponent to maintain distance. You can now stand all the way up without ever having lost your base. Make sure you are not too far away or too close to the opponent when you stand up. Once you are on your feet you will need to pass around the opponent's legs and establish side mount. In order to pass around the opponent's legs, you can grab one of their ankles and pull it across your body or walk around and shoot in from the side. If the opponent tries to get up, immediately shoot in from the side and establish side mount.

Abbreviated Directions:

After the opponent is down, stand up in base by leaning onto your right elbow and bending your left knee. Extend your left arm as you post on your right hand and left foot. Swing your right leg behind your right hand and stand up. Finish by shooting in to establish side mount.

Fill In the Word:

A t o i d, s u i b b l o y r e a b y l k. E y l a a y p o y r h a l f. S y r l b y r h a s u. F b s i t e s m.

Linking Story:

Once the opponent falls a safe distance away from me, I stand up by leaning onto my right cheese covered elbow and fold my left leg like a teepee. I then place my right hand into the ground like a shovel. Now I balance on my right shovel hand and left teepee leg. My folded right pocketknife leg extends open and the blade sticks into the ground behind my right shovel hand. I now stand all the way up and my left arm turns into a yard stick to keep the opponent away. I grab the opponent's ankle monitor and pull it across my body to establish side control.

Fill In the Story:

Cheese, teepee, shovel, pocketknife blade, shovel, yard stick, and ankle monitor.

Lesson 29: Rear Takedown (top of right side dresser)

Visual:

A person falls backward off the top of the right side dresser.

Lesson 29-A: Rear Clinch (left side of right side dresser)

Visual:

A person with snake arms clinches a walnut with their snake mouth hands while turned around with their rear side facing me on the left side of the dresser.

Directions:

If your head gets trapped under the opponent's right armpit from the front clinch, immediately drive your head up and back toward the opponent's head trapping their right arm behind your head. Shuffle your feet around to the opponent's right rear side while burying your head into their back. Your left leg should be placed between the opponent's legs and slightly back. This will form a triangle position for base. Never cross your feet when you are shuffling because you can easily fall down if the opponent tries to get away. The bend of your right elbow should be tight around the opponent's waist. Your hands should be joined with an S grip that has your right thumb pressing into the opponent's abdomen. Only stay in this position for a couple seconds before initiating the rear takedown.

Abbreviated Directions:

If your head is under the opponent's right armpit from the front clinch position, drive their right arm up with the back of your head as you step around to their right rear side. Join your hands together with an S grip and press your right thumb into their abdomen. Finish with a rear takedown.

Fill In the Word:

I y h i u t o r a f t f c p, d t r a u w t b o y h a y s a t t r r s. J y h t w a s g a p y r t i t a. F w a r t.

Linking Story:

The opponent's right armpit is covered in snake oil and my head is stuck under it. My arms turn into snakes and wrap around the opponent. My hands turn into snake heads that bite each other and form an S grip. I'm wearing a motorcycle helmet with a sharp spike on top that I drive upward toward the back of the opponent's head trapping their right arm behind my head. Now I lower my spike helmet and place it into the opponent's back as I shuffle my feet around to the right rear side position. The ground is covered in playing cards that form a triangle shape with my left leg at the top of the triangle. I bend my cheesy right elbow snake arm tightly around the opponent's waist and let the thumb on my cheesy right snake hand press into their abdomen while maintaining an S grip with my other snake arm.

Fill In the Story:

Snake oil, snake hands, snake bite, helmet spike, cards, triangle, cheesy elbow, and cheesy thumb.

Lesson 29-B: Rear Takedown (right side of right side dresser)

Visual:

A person jumps backward off of the right side of the dresser. They have a shoestring tied around their right ankle that breaks the fall.

Directions:

From the rear clinch position take a small step toward the opponent's right foot with your right foot. Now place the sole of your left foot half on the back of the opponent's left Achilles tendon and half on the ground to trap it in place. If you cannot see the back of the opponent's left ankle, you will have to trap it by feel, or by estimating where you think it is. Shoot your hips back and sit down while pulling the opponent back over your straight left leg that is trapping their left foot. Roll the opponent all the way over and secure the modified mount. Make sure you tuck your left elbow in toward the front of your body as you land on your side.

Abbreviated Directions:

From the rear clinch position, place your right foot near their right foot and trap the back of their left heel with your left foot. Shoot your hips backward as you sit down and pull the opponent over your left leg with your left elbow tucked in. Finish by establishing a modified mount.

Fill In the Word:

F t r c p, p y r f n t r f a t t b o t l h w y l f. S y h b a y s d a p t o o y l l w y l e t i. F b e a m m.

Linking Story:

My right foot moves close enough to their right foot to get tied together with a shoelace. The sole of my left foot is covered in glue so I place it half on the opponent's left heel and half on the ground. A gun goes off in my back pocket which causes my hips to shoot backward. As my hips shoot back, I pull the opponent backward across my straight as an arrow left leg that is glued to the back of the opponent's heel. My cheesy left elbow stays tucked in front of my body as I sit down. We end up rolling over a large dinner roll before I end up sitting on a saddle that is cinched to their right side.

Fill In the Story:

Shoelace, glue, gunshot, arrow, cheese, dinner roll, and saddle.

Lesson 30: Haymaker Punch Defense (wall mirror)

Visual:

A football player is wearing boxing gloves on top of the mirror and is holding a pitchfork with a flake of hay stuck through the forks. His rear leg has a ball and chain attached to it.

Directions:

With your lead left leg facing the opponent's rear right leg, squat down, cover your face with your left arm, and shoot in under their punching right arm. Once the opponent's punching right arm has gone over your head, secure the rear clinch and take them down.

Abbreviated Directions:

With your left leg forward, squat down and block your face with your left arm as you shoot in under their right punching arm. Finish by establishing the rear clinch and take them down.

Fill In the Word:

W y l l f, s d a b y f w y l a a y s i u t r p a. F b e t r c a t t d.

Linking Story:

My lead left leg is attached to the opponent's rear right leg with a chain and shackle. If the opponent's rear right leg moves backward my lead left leg moves forward. The opponent's right arm turns into a pitchfork that he throws at my face. My legs turn into duck legs that squat down to avoid the punch. My left hand is wearing an oversized boxing glove to block their punch. As I duck down a grenade falls out of my back pocket and explodes causing me to shoot in toward the opponent. I slide in under the opponent's right armpit that is covered in oil and secure the rear clinch. I then complete a rear take down that kicks up dust.

Fill In the Story:

Shackle, pitchfork, duck, boxing glove, grenade, oil, and dust.

Lesson 31: Take the Back – Guard (laundry room door)

Visual:

A British guard with a four of spades card on his right forearm takes a piece of candy that is stuck to a baby's back on top of the laundry room door.

Directions:

If the opponent is standing in your guard with their right forearm pressing into your neck, grab the back of their right tricep with your left hand. Now turn your face toward the direction of their right elbow and flex your neck for protection. Use your guard to squeeze the opponent's waist as you push their body south with your legs. Push their right forearm off of your neck and lower them down with your legs so that their right arm rests on the right side of your neck. Hug the back of the opponent's neck with your left arm and clasp your hands together behind their back. Keep your head pressed close to the opponent's head as you hold them. Now uncross your feet and place your left foot on the ground to help shrimp your hips toward the left side. Adjust your grip so that the blade of your right wrist is now pressing against the opponent's neck. Once you have moved your hips as far to the left side as possible, re-hook your left leg around the opponent's back to prevent them from mounting you. With your left leg hooked onto the opponent's back, place your right leg flat on the ground. Hold your hand grip tight around the opponent's neck as you slide your right leg south. This will push the opponent's left knee out from underneath them and your right leg will end up between their legs. When the opponent tries to get back on their knees, quickly bend your right knee and rest it against the inside of their left thigh. If the opponent does not try to get back to their knees after they get flattened out, you can immediately take their back from that position. If the opponent is too heavy and you cannot get all the way under their leg, bend your right knee, and place it inside their left thigh from the space you created by pushing their left leg south. Once your right knee is inside their left thigh release your hand grip. Now reach across their back with your left hand and grab their upper torso or shirt. Bend your right arm at the elbow and tuck it in next to your rib cage. Roll onto your right bottom shoulder and balance on it. Place weight on your left leg hook as you pull your right leg out from underneath the opponent. Then place your right knee and hand on the ground to create a strong base. Sink in your leg hooks and establish an over-under grip to complete the back mount.

Abbreviated Directions:

If the opponent has their right forearm on your neck, push them south with your legs and push their arm off your neck. Hug their neck and shrimp your hips out with your left foot. Sweep their left leg and bend your right knee. Hook their left torso and place your weight onto your right shoulder. Pull your right leg out and finish by taking their back.

Fill In the Word:

I t o h t r f o y n, p t s w y l a p t a o y n. H t n a s y h o w y l f. S t l l a b y r k. H t l t a p y w o y r s. P y r l o a f b t t b.

Linking Story:

The opponent is in my guard with a four of spades playing card stuck to his right forearm and it's pressing into my throat. My right arm turns into a gorilla's arm that uses a thumbless grip to grab the back of the opponent's left arm that is not on my throat. I turn my head to face the opponent's right elbow that is pressing into my neck. I flex my neck until it turns into a steel dumbbell. I press my legs together and squeeze the opponent downward like I'm extending an accordion. The accordion blows the four of spades card off of my neck. Once the opponent's right forearm is off of my neck, I push his forearm over to the right side of my neck like I'm playing the violin and I contract my accordion legs. Now I clasp my hands together behind the opponent's neck like I've become a spider monkey. A scooter appears below my hips and rolls me out to the right side of the opponent. Now my bottom right leg unhooks from the opponent's back and turns into a broom that lays flat on the ground. The broom extends straight and sweeps out the opponent's left knee. My broom is now between the opponent's legs. When the opponent tries to get back to their knees my right broom leg turns into a rooster leg that cocks up and blocks their left thigh. If my right leg cannot sweep the opponent's leg all the way flat, I can cock my right rooster leg and block their left thigh with the space I created from the partial sweep. Once I have the opponent's left thigh blocked, I release my spider monkey grip from around their neck and extend my top left hand that has turned into a bear's paw across their back, and I dig my bear claws into their upper left torso or shirt. My bottom right armpit is now covered in glue, and it clamps down my cheese covered right elbow. Then my bottom right shoulder turns into a roller skate that I balance my weight on. Now a remote-controlled car appears under my bottom right knee and drives it out from under the opponent's body. My right arm turns into a shovel that digs into the ground for a strong base. Both of my legs now turn into sharp bailing hooks that I hook into the opponent's legs and establish an over under grip with my spider monkey arms to secure the back mount position.

Fill In the Story:

Four of spades, gorilla arm, dumbbell, accordion, violin, spider monkey, scooter, broom, rooster leg, bear claws, glue, cheese, roller skate, car, shovel, bailing hooks, and monkey.

Lesson 32: Guillotine Defense (cabinets above laundry sink)

Visual:

A football player with a dumbbell neck is pushing a guillotine blade into the cabinets over the laundry room sink with his left gorilla arm.

Directions:

If the opponent has you in a standing guillotine with their right arm, immediately flex your neck muscles. Then use a thumbless grip to grab their right wrist with your left hand and pull down to release the pressure. Tuck your chin in to prevent their right arm from getting under your chin. Use your right arm to reach over the opponent's left shoulder. Place your right hand as far down on the back of the opponent as possible. Shuffle your feet around to the opponent's left side and straddle their left leg. Pull down on your right arm that is over the opponent's left shoulder while you simultaneously sweep their left leg out using your right knee that is on their backside. Take small steps as you drive the opponent backward and down to the ground. If you are not able to straddle the opponent's left leg you can hook their left leg with your rear right leg and take them down to the ground. The first method is easier to control and provides a more efficient take down. With your head still trapped in a guillotine place your right forearm that was behind the opponent's back onto their neck. Then grab the back of the opponent's right shoulder with your right hand to form a pivot point for your right forearm. Press down on the opponent's neck until they let go of the guillotine. You can saw back and forth with your forearm, punch the opponent in the face, or knee them in the head if needed. Whatever it takes to get your head out of the guillotine. Once your head is free establish an over under grip and establish the side mount position.

Abbreviated Directions:

From a right arm standing guillotine position, tuck your chin and pull down on their right wrist with your left hand. Hook your right arm over their left shoulder and step around to their left side. Pull down on their left shoulder as you sweep their left knee and take them down. Break their guillotine with your right forearm and establish side mount.

Fill In the Word:

F a r a s g p, t y c a p d o t r w w y l h. H y r a o t l s a s a t t l s. P d o t l s a y s t l k a t t d. B t g w y r f a e s m.

Linking Story:

The opponent has me in a standing guillotine choke with their right blade arm which causes my neck to turn into a steel dumbbell. My left arm turns into a gorilla's arm, and I pull down on the opponent's right arm until steam is released from my neck. I have glue under my chin that causes my chin to get stuck down to my neck. My right hand turns into a bear's arm that I reach over the opponents left shoulder and dig into their back. A deck of playing cards is scattered on the ground so I shuffle my feet across them and end up straddling the opponent's left leg that has turned into a tree. My right knee that is behind the opponent's left tree leg turns into an axe that I use to cut their left leg in half as I pull down on their left shoulder with my right bear arm. I take small steps across pebbles as I lower the opponent down to the ground. Now I take my right bear arm and place it across the opponent's neck and dig my claws into the back of their right shoulder to create a pivot point for my right forearm. I press down on the opponent's neck until honey comes out of their nose and they let go of the choke. I then secure an over under grip like a spider monkey and establish side mount.

Fill In the Story:

Blade, dumbbell, gorilla, steam, glue, bear arm, cards, tree, axe, bear arm, pebbles, bear arm, bear claws, honey, and spider monkey.

Lesson 33-A: Elbow Escape - Side Mount (laundry room faucet)

Visual:

A person is climbing down a fire escape with their elbows from the laundry room sink faucet and they get onto a horse sideways at the bottom of the sink bowl. The horses right shin is made from a banana.

Directions:

If the opponent slides their right leg across your abdomen from side mount, tuck your right elbow in and slide your right knee north. As the opponent's right knee gets close to touching the ground push their left knee over your right leg with your right elbow and trap it with your right leg. Now hug the back of the opponent's neck with your right arm. Use your left arm to brace against the opponent's right knee and push your hips out to the right side. This will give you enough space to bend your left knee toward the sky in front of the opponent's right thigh. Now hook the opponent's back with your right leg and scoot your hips toward the left side. This will give you enough space to swing your left leg around the opponent's right leg. Finish by crossing your legs behind the opponent's back to establish a closed guard position.

Abbreviated Directions:

As the opponent transitions into top mount, push their left knee over your right leg and trap it. Hug their neck and brace your left hand against their right knee. Shrimp your hips toward your right side and bend your left knee upright. Hook their back and shrimp your hips toward your left side. Swing your left leg around their right leg and finish by crossing your legs behind their back.

Fill In the Word:

A t o t i t m, p t l k o y r l a t i. H t n a b y l h a t r k. S y h t y r s a b y l k u. H t b a s y h t y l s. S y l l a t r l a f b c y l b t b.

Linking Story:

The opponent is on my right side in the side mount position, and they are sliding their right banana shin across my abdomen to establish top mount. My left knee turns into a teepee that I use to push my bodyweight onto my right knee that is a frozen popsicle sliding north along the ground. I tuck my right cheese covered elbow in close to my body. The cheesy right elbow catches on fire as it pushes the opponent's left knee south. The opponent now slides their right banana shin all the way across my abdomen and their right knee presses a red button on the ground that triggers an airbag to go off under my cheese covered right elbow. The force of the blast pushes my cheesy right elbow against the opponent's left knee so hard that it pushes their posted left knee over my right popsicle knee. Now my right popsicle knee turns into a teepee that I use to trap the opponent's left leg with. I use my cheese covered right arm to wrap around the back of the opponent's neck and I use my left arm that is wearing a red elbow brace to push against their right knee. Now a scooter appears below my hips, and it scoots my hips to the left side. This gives me enough room to slide my left teepee leg in front of the opponent's right thigh. Now my right teepee leg that is trapping the opponent's left leg turns into a bailing hook that sticks into the opponent's back. The scooter under my hips now goes back the other way toward my left teepee leg. This gives me enough room to swing my left teepee leg around the opponent's right leg. Now my left teepee leg turns into a bailing hook that I cross behind the opponent's back to establish a closed guard.

Fill In the Story:

Banana, teepee, popsicle, cheesy elbow, airbag, teepee, cheesy neck, red brace, scooter, teepee, bailing hook, scooter, and bailing hook.

Lesson 33-B: High Step Variation (sink drain)

Visual:

A nun high steps around the sink drain as she holds her arms in a V formation.

Directions:

If the opponent is in a reverse cross chest position on your right side, wait for them to step over your abdomen. Once their right knee gets close to touching the ground, use your right elbow and knee to push their left leg over your right leg. Finish with the standard variation from here.

Abbreviated Directions:

From the right side reverse cross chest position, push their left leg over your right leg with your right elbow and knee when their right leg is close to touching the ground. Finish with the standard variation.

Fill In the Word:

F t r s r c c p, p t l l o y r l w y r e a k w t r l i c t t t g. F w t s v.

Linking Story:

A nun with a cross pendant on her chest is in a cross-chest position on my right side when she goes to step over my abdomen with her right leg that is in the shape of an airplane. As her right airplane knee is about to touchdown on my left side, I use my right cheese covered elbow and popsicle knee to push her left knee over my right oil covered leg. My right teepee leg traps her left leg and I finish with the standard variation.

Fill In the Story:

Nun, cross, pendant, airplane, cheese, popsicle, oil, and teepee.

Lesson 34: Standing Armlock (cabinets below sink)

Visual:

A person is standing with their arm handcuffed to the cabinets under the laundry room sink. They are giving me a thumbs down as they stand there.

Directions:

If the opponent has their right arm extended with their right hand grabbing your chest or throat, grab their right wrist with your right hand thumb down. Then grab the opponent's right wrist a little higher up with your left hand thumb down. Once you have securely grabbed the opponent's wrist take one big step backward with your right leg. If the opponent is pushing you backward, time your big step backward with the pace you are walking. Assertively pull and roll the opponent's right arm over as you turn away from them. With the opponent now facing your back, extend their right arm all the way out in front of you as you block them with your hips. If the opponent is holding your shirt when you pull, rip their arm away from it in one sudden movement. Now apply upward pressure on the opponent's right wrist as you apply downward pressure on their right arm with your left armpit. As you apply downward pressure with your left armpit, make sure your left elbow slides in front of your left knee, so that it does not get blocked by it. If the opponent slides too far forward, use your ribcage to apply downward pressure on their right arm instead of your armpit.

Abbreviated Directions:

If the opponent has their right hand on your chest, grab their right wrist with both hands and step backward with your right leg. Pull the opponent's extended right arm over as you turn away and block them with your hips. Finish by lowering your left armpit as you pull up on their right wrist.

Fill In the Word:

I t o h t r h o y c, g t r w w b h a s b w y r l. P t o e r a o a y t a a b t w y h. F b l y l a a y p u o t r w.

Linking Story:

The opponent has their right arm extended with their right bear trap hand on my chest or throat. The opponent's right armpit stinks so I give him a thumbs down as I grab his right wrist with my right hand. Then my left hand gives him a thumbs down before grabbing a little higher up on his right arm. My right leg turns into a sasquatch leg that takes one big step backward. The opponent's right arm turns into a big tootsie roll that I pull and roll over as I turn around and block him with a cinder block that is attached to my hip. Now the opponent's trapped right arm has a huge hot air balloon attached to their right wrist that is causing their arm to rise into the air. I clamp down on the opponent's cheese covered right elbow with a bear trap that is under my left armpit. My left elbow is wrapped in a banana peel that slides in front of my left knee as the cheese on the opponent's right elbow starts to steam from the downward pressure my bear trap left armpit is applying.

Fill In the Story:

Bear trap, thumbs, sasquatch, tootsie roll, cinder block, balloon, cheese, bear trap armpit, banana peel, and steam.

Lesson 35-A: Twisting Arm Control (cabinets above washer and dryer)

Visual:

A tornado is spinning around a mannequin arm that is holding a television remote control on top of the cabinets over the washer and dryer. A bear trap and sledgehammer get slung out of the spinning tornado.

Directions:

From the top mount position, pin the opponent's right hand down on the left side of their head with your right hand on their right wrist, and your left hand behind their right elbow. Press your chest down on their right arm and slide your left hand, palm up, behind their neck and grab the opponent's trapped right wrist. Then use your right hand as base and jump into a modified mount position. Now push down on the back of the opponent's right tricep with your right hand as you pull up on their right wrist with your straight left arm. This will force the opponent on to their left side in a modified mount position. Keep your hips postured up over opponent with your left foot angled slightly out to form a strong base. Push down on the back of the opponent's right tricep as you pull up on their right wrist to prevent them from escaping.

Abbreviated Directions:

From the top mount position, push the opponent's right arm across their throat and press your chest down on it. Slide your left hand behind their neck and grab their right wrist. Post on your right hand and jump into a modified mount. Push down on their right tricep as you pull up on their right wrist. Finish by posturing up over the opponent with your left foot angled out.

Fill In the Word:

F t t m p, p t o r a a t t a p y c d o i. S y l h b t n a g t r w. P o y r h a j i a m m. P d o t r t a y p u o t r w. F b p u o t o w y l f a o.

Linking Story:

From the top mount position my right hand turns into a bear trap that grabs the opponent's right wrist. My left hand turns into a sledgehammer that presses against the opponent's right tricep and pushes their right arm across their throat. Now my bear trap right hand pins the opponent's right hand down to the ground. Then I slam my chest that has a large elephant foot tattoo on it into the back of their cheese covered right elbow to keep their right arm pinned down. Then my left hand turns into a palm tree that I forcefully slide palm up behind the opponent's neck. Now my bear trap right hand turns into a bulldozer and pushes the opponent's right wrist over to my palm tree left hand. Now my palm tree left hand turns back into a bear trap that clamps down on the opponent's right wrist with a full grip. Now that my bulldozer right hand is free, it lowers its blade into the ground to create a solid base. My legs turn into frog legs, so I jump into a modified mount position. I then use my bulldozer right hand to push against the opponent's right tricep as my bear trap left hand raises the opponent's right wrist up toward the sky like it's being lifted by a large crane. Now I balance a book on my head as I keep my hips postured up over the opponent. My left leg extends out for base just like the jack on a crane. Once the opponent is on their left side in a modified amount position, I keep my heavy equipment in place for a few seconds before working submissions.

Fill In the Story:

Bear trap, hammer, elephant, cheese, palm tree, bulldozer, bear trap, blade, frog, bulldozer, crane, book, and jack.

Lesson 35-B: Back Mount Submission (washer)

Visual:

A person is eating a tootsie roll as they ride a horse bareback on top of a submarine that is docked inside the wash machine.

Directions:

From the twisting arm control position, wait for the opponent to try rolling over to get on their knees. Once they start to roll over let go of their twisted arm and use both of your hands as base. When they get up on their knees shoot your hooks in and establish the back mount. From the back you can finish the opponent with a rear naked choke.

Abbreviated Directions:

From the twisting arm control position, let go of their arm and post on your hands if they roll over. When they get up on their knees, establish leg hooks, and finish with a rear naked choke.

Fill In the Word:

F t t a c p, l g o t a a p o y h i t r o. W t g u o t k, e l h, a f w a r n c.

Linking Story:

The opponent starts to roll over on top of a tootsie roll so my arms let go of their twisted pretzel arm and they turn into shovels that dig into the ground to form a strong base. Once they roll over to their red knee pads my legs turn into sharp bailing hooks that hook their legs and secure a back mount position. My arms then turn into snakes that wrap around their neck to choke them out.

Fill In the Story:

Tootsie roll, pretzel, shovels, knee pads, bailing hooks, and snakes.

Lesson 35-C: Armlock Submission (dryer)

Visual:

A person with a left crane arm and a bulldozer right hand is handcuffed to a submarine that is docked on top of the dryer.

Directions:

If the opponent does not try to roll over from the modified mount position, you can initiate an armlock. Loosen the opponent's right arm that is twisted under their neck by pushing it far enough forward to create a gap. Now slide your right hand through the gap and grab your left wrist that is holding the opponent's right wrist. Walk your right foot that is in front of the opponent's abdomen north until your right heel is next to their chest. Then bend your right knee south to create the angle needed to finish the armlock. Unhook your left arm from behind the opponent's neck and pivot off of your hands that are pressing the opponent's right hand down into the ground. Swing your left leg that is behind the opponent's back around the opponent's head and finish with an armlock.

Abbreviated Directions:

If the opponent does not roll over from the modified mount position, push their right arm forward and grab your left wrist with your right hand. Walk your right foot north and open your right hip. Unhook your left arm from behind their head and post on your hands. Swing your left leg around their head and finish with an armlock.

Fill In the Word:

I t o d n r o f t m m p, p t r a f a g y l w w y r h. W y r f n a o y r h. U y l a f b t h a p o y h. S y l l a t h a f w a a.

Linking Story:

If the opponent stays in the modified mount position and I'm sitting in a saddle on their right side, I will lower my left crane arm down and push their right wrist back across their neck. This will create a gap that my bulldozer right hand can plow through. Once my bulldozer right hand gets through the gap it turns into a bear trap that clamps down on my own left wrist that is still holding the opponent's right wrist. My right foot that is next to the opponent's abdomen has a dog leash attached to it as it walks up next to their chest. Once my right foot gets next to their chest my right knee slams down to the ground and cracks my right hip like a turkey wishbone. Now I unhook my left arm from behind the opponent's oily neck and press all of my body weight onto their right hand, like I'm pressing a nail into the ground. I pivot on my hands as I swing my left rear leg around their head like a helicopter blade and I finish the armlock.

Fill In the Story:

Saddle, crane, bulldozer, bear trap, dog leash, wishbone, oil, nail, and helicopter blade.

Lesson 36: Double Underhook Guard Pass (cabinet top on the right side of dryer)

Visual:

A British guard with a large marshmallow on his abdomen is wearing a backstage pass around his neck and is using his hook arms to slide under the cabinet top.

Directions:

From the opponent's closed guard, sit back and press your hands into their abdomen. Now punch the opponent in the abdomen to open their guard. Then pull your arms back and establish double under hooks. Push the opponent's legs forward as you hook their left shoulder with your left hand. Step around to their right side as you posture up and let their legs slide down the front of your torso. Finish by establishing a modified side mount.

Abbreviated Directions:

From the opponent's closed guard, sit back and punch them in the abdomen to open their guard. Pull your arms backward and establish double underhooks. Push their legs forward as you hook their left shoulder with your left hand. Step around to their right side as you posture up and let their legs slide down the front of your torso. Finish by establishing a modified side mount.

Fill In the Word:

F t o c g, s b a p t i t a t o t g. P y a b a e d u. P t l f a y h t l s w y l h. S a t t r s a y p u a l t l s d t f o y t. F b e a m s m.

Linking Story:

The opponent has me in their closed guard, so I push both of my hands into their marshmallow abdomen. Then I posture up on my knees that are resting on books. My hands have oversized boxing gloves on that I use to punch the opponent with. Once the opponent uncrosses their legs, my arms turn into bailing hooks that tuck in like turtle legs before hooking the opponent's legs. The opponent's right leg turns into a sack of potatoes, so I slide my left shoulder under it. Now I lean forward on red knee pads, and then onto my toes, as I push the sack of potatoes toward the opponent's left shoulder. Once my left arm is close enough, I hook the opponent's left shoulder with my bailing hook left hand and press my left forearm across their throat. Now I step across a ladder that is on the ground while I press my weight into the opponent's throat and legs. My legs are wide apart with my right southern leg on fire and my northern leg frozen like a popsicle in a northwest direction. A book appears on my head, so I posture up to keep it from falling which causes the sack of potatoes to slide down in front of my face. Now I slide my left forearm across the opponent's throat and place my cheese covered left elbow on the ground next to their neck. My right forearm is made of steel and is stuck to a magnet that is in the ground under the opponent's right thigh. I keep my head low to avoid getting stung by bees that are flying over my head. I now place my chest on the opponent's chest, as a huge elephant steps on my back. My southern right knee has a fiery spear tip on it that I stick into the opponent's waist. My left leg is a popsicle that stays in a northwest direction with my toes touching the ground. I have steel weights in my pants back pockets that keep my hips low to the ground.

Fill In the Story:

Marshmallow, books, boxing gloves, bailing hooks, turtle, potatoes, knee pads, bailing hook, ladder, book, potatoes, cheese, magnet, bees, elephant, spear, popsicle, and pocket weights.

References

REF 1. R. Douglas Fields (2020) The Brain Learns in Unexpected Ways, *Scientific American* 322, 3, 74-79

REF 2. Ericsson, Chase & Faloon, (1980)

REF 3. *Jonides, Lewis, Nee, Lustig, Berman, Moore, Sledge (2008) The Mind and Brain of Short-Term Memory, Annual Review of Psychology 193–224*

REF 4. *O'Keefe, Dostrovsky (1971) The Hippocampus as a Spatial Map, Brain Research 171-175*

REF 5. Pan, Mayoral, Choi (2020) Preservation of a Remote Fear Memory Requires New Myelin Formation. *Nature Neuroscience 487–499*

REF 6. *Trafton (2017) Neuroscientists Identify Brain Circuit Necessary for Memory Formation., MIT News Office*

REF 7. Sperry (2011) The Split Brain Experiments, *Nobelprize. org*

REF 8. Guy-Evans (2021) Lateralization of Brain Function

REF 9. Healy (2013) Einsteins's Brain Really Was Bigger Than Most People's, *Los Angeles Times*

REF 10. *Giorgi, Federico (2020) Gene Network Reverse Engineering, The Next Generation*

REF 11. *Pillay (2011) The Science of Visualization, Huff Post*

REF 12. *Burch, Donner M.D. (2022) When Do Babies Start Walking?, Baby Center*

REF 13. Zajonc (2001) Mere Exposure: A Gateway to the Subliminal, *Current Directions in Psychological Science*

REF 14. Augustine, Fitzpatrick (2001) Neuroscience Second Edition, *Sinauer Associates*

REF 15. Delorme, Poncet, Fabre-Thorp (2018) Briefly Flashed Scenes Can Be Stored in Long-Term Memory, *Frontiers in Neuroscience*

REF 16. Barragan-Jason, Lachat, Barbeau, (2012) How Fast is Famous Face Recognition? *Frontiers in Psychology*

REF 17. Bonin, Gelin, Bugaiska (2013) Animates Are Better Remembered Than Inanimates: Further Evidence from Word and Picture Stimuli., *Memory & Cognition* 42 pgs. 370-382

REF 18. Brady, T. F., Konkle, T., Alvarez, G. A., and Oliva, A. (2008) Visual long-term memory has a massive storage capacity for object details., *Proc. Natl. Acad. Sci.* U.S.A. 105, 14325–14329

REF 19. Brady, T. F., Konkle, T., Oliva, A., and Alvarez, G. A. (2009) Detecting changes in real-world objects: The relationship between visual long-term memory and change blindness. *Communicative & Integrative Biology* 2, 1–3

REF 20. Bugelski, B. R. (1962) Presentation time, total time, and mediation in paired-associate learning. *Journal of Experimental Psychology* 63, 409–412

REF 21. Cooper, E. H., and Pantle, A. J. (1967) The total-time hypothesis in verbal learning., *Psychological Bulletin* 68, 221–234

REF 22. Curran, T. (2000). Brain potentials of recollection and familiarity. *Memory & Cognition* 28, 923–938

REF 23. Curran, T., and Cleary, A. M. (2003) Using ERPs to dissociate recollection from familiarity in picture recognition. *Cognitive Brain Research* 15, 191–205

REF 24. Curran, T., and Doyle, J. (2011) Picture superiority doubly dissociates the ERP correlates of recollection and familiarity. *J. Cogn. Neurosci.* 23, 1247–1262

REF 25. Donaldson, W., Mackenzie, T. M., and Underhill, C. F. (1996) A comparison of recollective memory and source monitoring. *Psychonomic Bulletin & Review* 3, 486–490

REF 26. Ecker, U. K. H., and Zimmer, H. D. (2009) ERP evidence for flexible adjustment of retrieval orientation and its influence on familiarity. *J. Cogn. Neurosci.* 21, 1907–1919

REF 27. Ecker, U. K. H., Zimmer, H. D., Groh-Bordin, C., and Mecklinger, A. (2007) Context effects on familiarity are familiarity effects of context - an electrophysiological study. *International Journal of Psychophysiology* 64, 146–156

REF 28. Endress, A. D., and Potter, M. C. (2012) Early Conceptual and Linguistic Processes Operate in Independent Channels. *Psychological Science* 23, 235–245

REF 29. Fabre-Thorpe, M., Delorme, A., Marlot, C., and Thorpe, S. (2001) A limit to the speed of processing in ultra-rapid visual categorization of novel natural scenes. *J. Cogn. Neurosci.* 13, 171–180

REF 30. Glen, F., Smith, N. D., and Crabb, D. P. (2013) Saccadic eye movements and face recognition performance in patients with central glaucomatous visual field defects. *Vision Research.* *Volume* 82, 19. April 2013, Pages 42–51

REF 31. Gonsalves, B. D., Kahn, I., Curran, T., Norman, K. A., and Wagner, A. D. (2005) Memory strength and repetition suppression: multimodal imaging of medial temporal cortical contributions to recognition. *Neuron* 47, 751–761

REF 32. Groh-Bordin, C., Zimmer, H. D., and Mecklinger, A. (2005) Feature binding in perceptual priming and in episodic object recognition: evidence from event-related brain potentials. *Cognitive Brain Research* 24, 556–567

REF 33. Hipp, J., and Siegel, M. (2013) Dissociating neuronal gamma-band activity from cranial and ocular muscle activity in EEG. *Front Hum Neurosci.* 2013:338

REF 34. Hollingworth, A., and Henderson, J. M. (2002) Accurate visual memory for previously attended objects in natural scenes. *Journal of Experimental Psychology* 28, 113–136

REF 35. Huebner, G. M., and Gegenfurtner, K. R. (2012) Conceptual and Visual Features Contribute to Visual Memory for Natural Images.

REF 36. Intraub, H. (1979) The role of implicit naming in pictorial encoding. *Journal of Experimental Psychology* 5, 78–87

REF 37. Intraub, H. (1980) Presentation rate and the representation of briefly glimpsed pictures in memory. *Journal of Experimental Psychology. Human Learning and Memory* 6, 1–12

REF 38. Konkle, T., Brady, T. F., Alvarez, G. A., and Oliva, A. (2010) Conceptual distinctiveness supports detailed visual long-term memory for real-world objects. *J. Exp. Psychol. Gen.* 139, 558–578

REF 39. Konkle, T., Brady, T. F., Alvarez, G. A., and Oliva, A. (2010) Scene memory is more detailed than you think: the role of categories in visual long-term memory. *Psychological Science* 21, 1551–1556

REF 40. Koutstaal, W., and Schacter, D. L. (1997) Gist-Based False Recognition of Pictures in Older and Younger Adults. *Journal of Memory and Language* 37, 555–583

REF 41. Küper, K., Groh-Bordin, C., Zimmer, H. D., and Ecker, U. K. H. (2012) Electrophysiological correlates of exemplar-specific processes in implicit and explicit memory. *Cognitive, Affective & Behavioral Neuroscience* 12, 52–64

REF 42. Li, F. F., VanRullen, R., Koch, C., and Perona, P. (2002) Rapid natural scene categorization in the near absence of attention. *Proc. Natl. Acad. Sci. U.S.A.* 99, 9596–9601

REF 43. Loftus, G. R. (1972) Eye fixations and recognition memory for pictures. *Cognit. Psychol.* 3, 525–551

REF 44. Lucas, H. D., Taylor, J. R., Henson, R. N., and Paller, K. A. (2012) Many roads lead to recognition: Electrophysiological correlates of familiarity derived from short-term masked repetition priming. *Neuropsychologia* 50, 3041–3052

REF 45. Martini, P., and Maljkovic, V. (2009) Short-term memory for pictures seen once or twice. *Vision Research* 49, 1657–1667

REF 46. Mecklinger, A., Frings, C., and Rosburg, T. (2012) Response to Paller et al.: the role of familiarity in making inferences about unknown quantities. *Trends in Cognitive Sciences* 16, 315–316

REF 47. Melcher, D. (2001) Persistence of visual memory for scenes. *Nature* 412, 401–401

REF 48. Melcher, D., and Kowler, E. (2001) Visual scene memory and the guidance of saccadic eye movements. *Vision Research* 41, 3597–3611

REF 49. Melcher, D., and Murphy, B. (2011) The role of semantic interference in limiting memory for the details of visual scenes. *Frontiers in Psychology* 2:262

REF 50. Nairne, J. S., Pandeirada, J. N. S., and Thompson, S. R. (2008) Adaptive memory: the comparative value of survival processing. *Psychological Science* 19, 176–180

REF 51. Nairne, J. S., Vanarsdall, J. E., Pandeirada, J. N. S., Cogdill, M., and Lebreton, J. M. (2013) Adaptive memory: the mnemonic value of animacy. *Psychological Science* 24, 2099–2105

REF 52. Paller, K. A., Lucas, H. D., and Voss, J. L. (2012) Assuming too much from 'familiar'brain potentials. *Trends in cognitive sciences* 16, 313–315

REF 53. Paller, K. A., Voss, J. L., and Boehm, S. G. (2007) Validating neural correlates of familiarity. *Trends in Cognitive Sciences* 11, 243–250

REF 54. Potter, M. C. (1976) Short-term conceptual memory for pictures. Journal of Experimental Psychology. *Human Learning and Memory* 2, 509–522

REF 55. Ranganath, C., DeGutis, J., and D'Esposito, M. (2004) Category-specific modulation of inferior temporal activity during working memory encoding and maintenance. *Brain Res. Cogn. Brain Res* 2004, 37–45

REF 56. Rissman, J., Greely, H. T., and Wagner, A. D. (2010) Detecting individual memories through the neural decoding of memory states and past experience. *Proc. Natl. Acad. Sci. U.S.A.* 107, 9849–9854

REF 57. Rousselet, G. A., Thorpe, S. J., and Fabre-Thorpe, M. (2004) Processing of one, two or four natural scenes in humans: the limits of parallelism. *Vision Research* 44, 877–894

REF 58. Rugg, M. D., and Curran, T. (2007) Event-related potentials and recognition memory. *Trends in Cognitive Sciences* 11, 251–257

REF 59. Schloerscheidt, A. M., and Rugg, M. D. (1997) Recognition memory for words and pictures: An event-related potential study. *NeuroReport* 8, 3281–3284

REF 60. Schloerscheidt, A. M., and Rugg, M. D. (2004) The impact of change in stimulus format on the electrophysiological indices of recognition. *Neuropsychologia* 42, 451–466

REF 61. Shaffer, W., and Shiffrin, R. M. (1972) Rehearsal and storage of visual information. *Journal of Experimental Psychology* 92, 292–296

REF 62. Shepard, R. N. (1967) Recognition memory for words, sentences, and pictures. *Journal of Verbal Learning and Verbal Behavior* 6, 156–163

REF 63. Snodgrass, J. G., and Corwin, J. (1988) Pragmatics of measuring recognition memory: applications to dementia and amnesia. *J. Exp. Psychol. Gen.* 117, 34–50

REF 64. Squire, L. R., Wixted, J. T., and Clark, R. E. (2007) Recognition memory and the medial temporal lobe: a new perspective. *Nature Reviews. Neuroscience* 8, 872–883

REF 65. Standing, L. (1973) Learning 10,000 pictures. *The Quarterly Journal of Experimental Psychology* 25, 207–222

REF 66. Standing, L., Conezio, J., and Haber, R. N. (1970) Perception and memory for pictures: Single-trial learning of 2500 visual stimuli. *Psychonomic Science* 19, 73–74

REF 67. Tatler, B. W., Gilchrist, I. D., and Rusted, J. (2003) The time course of abstract visual representation. *Perception* 32, 579–592

REF 68. Thorpe, S. J., Fize, D., and Marlot, C. (1996) Speed of processing in the human visual system. *Nature* 381, 520–522

REF 69. Tsivilis, D., Otten, L. J., and Rugg, M. D. (2001) Context effects on the neural correlates of recognition memory: an electrophysiological study. *Neuron* 31, 497–505

REF 70. Tsuchiya, N., and Koch, C. (2016) "The Neurology of Conciousness," in *Cognitive Neuroscience and Neuropathology*, 2nd Edn, eds S. Laureys, O. Gosseries, and G. Tononi (New York, NY: Elsevier)

REF 71. VanArsdall, J. E., Nairne, J. S., Pandeirada, J. N. S., and Blunt, J. R. (2013) Adaptive memory: animacy processing produces mnemonic advantages. *Exp. Psychol.* 60, 172–178

REF 72. VanRullen, R., and Thorpe, S. J. (2001) The time course of visual processing: from early perception to decision-making. *J. Cogn. Neurosci.* 13, 454–461

REF 73. Vilberg, K. L., Moosavi, R. F., and Rugg, M. D. (2006) The relationship between electrophysiological correlates of recollection and amount of information retrieved. *Brain Research* 1122, 161–170

REF 74. Vilberg, K. L., and Rugg, M. D. (2009) Functional significance of retrieval-related activity in lateral parietal cortex: Evidence from fMRI and ERPs. *Hum. Brain Mapp.* 30, 1490–1501

REF 75. Vogt, S., and Magnussen, S. (2007) Long-term memory for 400 pictures on a common theme. *Exp. Psychol.* 54, 298–303

REF 76. Voss, J. L., and Federmeier, K. D. (2011) FN400 potentials are functionally identical to N400 potentials and reflect semantic processing during recognition testing. *Psychophysiology* 48, 532–546

REF 77. Voss, J. L., and Paller, K. A. (2006) Fluent Conceptual Processing and Explicit Memory for Faces Are Electrophysiologically Distinct. *J. Neurosci.* 26, 926–933

REF 78. Voss, J. L., Schendan, H. E., and Paller, K. A. (2010) Finding meaning in novel geometric shapes influences electrophysiological correlates of repetition and dissociates perceptual and conceptual priming. *NeuroImage* 49, 2879–2889

REF 79. Wiesmann, M., and Ishai, A. (2008) Recollection- and familiarity-based decisions reflect memory strength. *Frontiers in Systems Neuroscience* 2:1

REF 80. Wiseman, S., and Neisser, U. (1974) Perceptual organization as a determinant of visual recognition memory. *Am. J. Psychol.* 87, 675–681

REF 81. Wixted, J. T. (2007) Dual-process theory and signal-detection theory of recognition memory. *Psychological Review* 114, 152–176

REF 82. Yago, E., and Ishai, A. (2006) Recognition memory is modulated by visual similarity. *NeuroImage* 31, 807–817

REF 83. Yonelinas, A. P. (1994) Receiver-operating characteristics in recognition memory: evidence for a dual-process model. *Journal of Experimental Psychology.* 20, 1341–1354

REF 84. Yonelinas, A. P., Otten, L. J., Shaw, K. N., and Rugg, M. D. (2005) Separating the brain regions involved in recollection and familiarity in recognition memory. *The Journal of Neuroscience* 25, 3002–3008

REF 85. Yu, S. S., and Rugg, M. D. (2010) Dissociation of the electrophysiological correlates of familiarity strength and item repetition. *Brain Res.* 1320, 74–84

REF 86. Zimmer, H. D., and Ecker, U. K. H. (2010) Remembering perceptual features unequally bound in object and episodic tokens: Neural mechanisms and their electrophysiological correlates. *Neuroscience & Biobehavioral Reviews* 34, 1066–1079

REF 87. *Dresler, M.; Shirer, W. R.; Konrad, B. N.; Wagner, I. C.; Fernández, F.; Czisch, M.; Greicius, M. D. (2017) Mnemonic Training Reshapes Brain Networks to Support Superior Memory. Neuron, 93, 1227–1235*

REF 88. *O'Day, D. H. (2007) The Value of Animations in Biology Teaching: A Study of Long-Term Memory Retention. CBE Life Science Education, Fall 6: 217-223*

REF 89. *Amunts K, Kedo O, Kindler M, Pieperhoff P, Mohlberg H, Shah NJ, Habel U, Schneider F, Zilles K (2005) Cytoarchitectonic Mapping of the Human Amygdala, Hippocampal Region and Entorhinal Cortex: Inter-subject Variability and Probability Maps. Anatomy and Embryology, 210 (5–6): 343 (52)*

REF 90. Heuer, F. & Reisberg, D. (2007) The memory effects of emotion, stress and trauma. In D. Ross, M. Toglia, R. Lindsay, & D. Read (Eds.), *Handbook of eyewitness psychology: Volume 1 – Memory for events, 81-116*

REF 91. Teubner, Leipzig, (1923) Rhetorica ad Herennium, *Friedrich Marx Edition*

REF 92. Katona, G. A., (1975) Psychological Economics, *New York, NY: Elsevier*

REF 93. Diemer J, Muhlberger A, Pauli P, et al. (2014) Virtual reality exposure in anxiety disorders: Impact on psychophysiological reactivity. *World J Biol Psychiatry* 15: 427–442

REF 94. Rangachari, Devika (2011) Swami Vivekananda: A Man with a Vision, *Penguin Books Limited*, Page 21

REF 95. Lamb, Pugh (2006) Phototransduction, Dark Adaptation, and Rhodopsin Regeneration,

Investigative Ophthalmology & Visual Science, Vol.47, 5138-5152

REF 96. Ullman, MT (2004) Contributions of memory circuits to language: the declarative/procedural model, *Cognition.* 92 (1–2): 231–70

REF 97. Tulving E, Schacter DL, Stark HA (1982) Priming Effects in Word Fragment Completion are independent of Recognition Memory., *Journal of Experimental Psychology: Learning, Memory, and Cognition.* 8 (4): 336–342

REF 98-A. Nelson, T.O (1990) Metamemory: A theoretical framework and new findings., The Psychology of Learning and Motivation. *Vol 26. Academic Press.* pp. 125-173

REF 98-B. Umejima, Ibaraki, Yamazaki, Sakai, (2021) Paper Notebooks vs. Mobile Devices: Brain Activation Differences During Memory Retrieval., *Frontiers in Behavioral Neuroscience, Sec. Learning and Memory,* Volume 15

REF 99. Johnson, A. Michael (1990) Speed of Mental Rotation as a Function of Problem-Solving Strategies, *Perceptual and Motor Skills,* pgs. 803-806

REF 100. Sluming, V., Brooks, J., Howard, M., Downes, J. J., & Roberts, N. (2007) Broca's area supports enhanced visuospatial cognition in orchestral musicians. *The Journal of Neuroscience*, pgs. 3799–3806

REF 101. Pietsch, S., & Jansen, P. (2012) Different mental rotation performance in students of music, sport and education. *Learning and Individual Differences,* pgs.159–163

REF 102. Kim Peek (2008) The Real Rain Man, *Wisconsin Medical Society*

REF 103. Costandi, Moheb (2016) Neuroplasticity, *MIT Press*

REF 104. Avery C., Zemsky P., (1998) Multi-dimensional uncertainty and herd behavior in financial markets. *Amer. Econ. Rev.* 88, 724–748

Index

Memory Techniques:

Jiu-Jitsu Techniques:

Notes

NOTES

Printed in Great Britain
by Amazon